Top, Blackberry Jam Cake, page 147; left, Pizza de Ocean, page 146; right, *Alaria* Roll-ups, page 87; bottom, *Gracileria* Ogo Salad, page 116.

SEA VEGETABLES

harvesting guide
&
cookbook

EVELYN McCONNAUGHEY

Naturegraph

Library of Congress Cataloging in Publication Data

McConnaughey, Evelyn
  Sea Vegetables.

  Bibliography: p.
  Includes index.
    1. Marine algae as food.   2. Cookery (Marine algae)
3. Marine algae.   I. Title.
TX402.M33   1985   641.3   85-18828
ISBN 0-87961-150-2
ISBN 0-87961-151-0 (pbk.)

Drawings by Wendy Lou Manley

NATUREGRAPH PUBLISHERS, INC.
P.O. Box 1075
Happy Camp, California 96039
U.S.A.

Books for a better world

CONTENTS

Part I — The World of Seaweeds

Part II — From Shore to Stove

Part III — Seaweeds in Society

ILLUSTRATIONS

PHOTOGRAPHS

TABLES

Experimental nori culture in Puget Sound.

ACKNOWLEDGEMENTS

*Men who fish, botanize, work
with the turning-lathe, or gather
seaweeds, will make admirable
husbands.*
                    Robert Louis Stevenson

To my long-suffering husband, Bayard,
who not only gathers seaweed, but eagerly
sampled all the cooking experiments.

Strangely enough, support for this endeavor came from individuals not converted to eating sea vegetables, as well as those who were. I am especially grateful to those friends who stuck with me even if they didn't understand what all the eagerness and enthusiasum over seaweed was about. I am most indebted to my marine biologist spouse, our five children, and my parents, who are always ready to take on any challenge— the more "far out" the better.

Dr. Ed Lippert, marine botanist, introduced me to the idea of eating seaweed. Though she wouldn't touch seaweed cooking, Jean Hanna, doughty librarian, technician and all-around good sport at the University of Oregon's Institute of Marine Biology (OIMB), thought this book was a great idea; and she encouraged and helped with the writing. Staff members at OIMB, including Lynn Rudy, artist, and her husband Paul, director, and the Terwillegers, Bob and Nora, also tolerated the effort. Marge Lebow, OIMB Secretary, cheerfully typed and retyped the many drafts. Some of the students at OIMB were my best missionaries. Mike Graybill and Jan Hodder undertook the layout and printing of the first recipe booklet, and offered encouragement with recipes.

I especially am grateful to Dr. Bob Waaland, phycologist and author of *Common Seaweeds of the Pacific Northwest,* who scrutinized the manuscript, and to Dr. Tom Mumford, Washington State Department of Natural Resources, who contributed a lot to my understanding of the biology of seaweeds and economics of seaweed farming.

Many others encouraged me, especially our children: Bill, who introduced me to Madlener's recipe book; Ted and John, both making careers in marine biology, and who help collect seaweed; Diane, who inspired some of the vegetarian recipes; and Becky, who helped with recipes, calligraphy, proofreading, labeling and marketing, and used seaweed motifs in batiking my demonstration accouterments. Jim Springer helped edit and proofread, and built our solar greenhouse seaweed dryer—probably the world's first.

It would be impossible to list all the people brave enough to try my recipes and offer suggestions, but I must mention Cameron Hubbe and Martha Wagner, who shared their recipes. Others who helped in various ways include Bill Shurtleff, co-author of several books on tempeh and tofu; Luke Lukoskie, of American Sea Vegetable Company; Peggy Robinson, author of *Profiles of Northwest Plants,* who read and commented on the manuscript; Lou Walker and Andrea Coffman, who helped with references from the University of Oregon Science and Law libraries; Jeanne Culbertson, extension agent and seaweed proselytizer from Alaska, who shared recipes and experiences; and Dr. Ron Phillips, who expanded my understanding of the complexities of marine coastal ecosystems. Finally, I wish to express my gratitude to the illustrator of the book, Wendy Lou Manley, whose own appreciation of the outdoors is reflected in her artwork.

PREFACE

*The sea is the lands' edge. Also the granite
Into which it reaches, the beaches where it tosses
Its hints of earlier and other creations:
The starfish, the hermit crab, the whales' backbone;
The pools where it offers to our curiosity
The more delicate algae and the sea anenome
It tosses up our losses, the torn sieve,
The shattered lobster pot, the broken oar
And the gear of foreign dead men. The sea
   has many voices.*

Eliot, *The Dry Salvages*

I have enjoyed many summers with my family at the University of Oregon's Institute of Marine Biology (OIMB) on the spectacular rocky Oregon coast. Accompanying my husband (a professor at OIMB) and his class on field trips, I at first perceived seaweed as something slippery and slimy and simply in the way of observing more fascinating marine invertebrates exposed at low tide. However, taking a course in marine algology, or phycology (the branch of botany dealing with algae), opened my eyes to the beauty of seaweeds, as well as to their importance to the ecosystem. Most importantly, the instructor introduced me to the culinary possibilities of seaweed by sharing a jar of his wife's kelp pickles.

Immediately, my cooking experiments began and were expanded by Judith Madlener's book on sea vegetable cooking. Though most sea vegetable recipes are based on Oriental cooking, I found seaweeds versatile and adaptable to all kinds of cuisines and recipes, from hors d'oeuvres to pizza. As any convert, I began proselytizing, demonstrating cooking techniques and leading foraging trips. This led to publishing a recipe booklet as a fund-raising venture to benefit OIMB. In writing this "how-to" book, featuring seaweeds in familiar and popular American recipes, I hope others will come to enjoy this tasty and nutritious contribution to health and natural foods menus.

Until recently, I had only seen one other person, an immigrant woman from Korea, gathering seaweed for food from the abundant algae forests of Oregon's coast. For centuries, Orientals have included seaweed as a vital part of their diets and cultures, attributing many healthful benefits to their use. Europeans, as well, have used seaweeds as foods, fertilizer and fodder. But surprisingly, this resource is largely ignored in the U.S., despite the fact that various extracts of seaweeds benefit many commercial food products from ice cream to beer; and most other food sources have long been harnessed, exploited and over-developed. Perhaps to the descendants of land-hugging farmers, seaweeds are not very obvious. And it is true, some planning and effort go into gathering seaweeds, and the forces of nature must be considered, which, in our civilized lives, we often ignore.

I truly believe an increased awareness of the economic potential of seaweeds will inspire all to maintain and enhance our beautiful sea forests. Certain commercial interests may become a positive force in preventing pollution and further degradation of the environment. Already research and development, as well as the cultivation of desired sea vegetable species, has been initiated in the U.S. and a viable industry in farming seaweeds is foretold. With careful planning, research, new laws, and thoughtful consideration of long-term effects on all forms of ocean life in developing this resource, future generations will enjoy the miracle of sea vegetables.

Documenting the numerous and diverse contributions of seaweeds to good health and the environment could easily result in an encyclopedia. But, my chief purpose here is to provide information about the more choice and abundant American seaweeds used in the diet. A thorough, yet concise, overview of seaweeds launches the book. The nutritional value of seaweed is given due attention, as well as the role of seaweed in the world hunger situation. For those ambitious and adventuresome individuals who wish to forage for their own sea vegetables, details on where to collect seaweeds, what kind to collect and most importantly, how to do it, precede the main section which describes and illustrates specific sea vegetables and how to prepare the delicious recipes in which they are used. And for those cooks who wish to try the recipes without necessarily embarking in the adventures of foraging, rest assured you won't miss out on these appealing and satisfying recipes as dried imported seaweeds may be substituted (see Table 6, page 64). In addition, recipes for popular imported and domestic commercial varieties of seaweeds will also be shared. Concluding the book, additional roles seaweeds play in society are discussed.

I hope to inspire the reader to include sea vegetables, this amazing creation of nature, in his/her own life for the purpose of better health, enjoyment and ultimately great satisfaction.

Part I

The World of Seaweeds

CHAPTER ONE

A WAITING BONANZA

Seaweeds: An Introduction

Seas and oceans cover over two-thirds of the world's surface and produce a large percentage of the earth's living resources; yet plants, the essential base of this production, are a largely unknown and undeveloped resource. Floating microscopic algae (phytoplankton), the "grass of the sea," produce 80 – 100 billion tons of carbohydrates annually, comparable to what is created by all plants on land. The edge of the sea is one of the richest habitats for plant growth in temperate latitudes. In the shallow coastal areas, the larger marine algae and seagrasses, commonly called seaweeds, may contribute three times the production of the phytoplankton. In primary production, these treasures of the sea growing as lush as a tropical rain forest, are largely unseen and unknown by most people, who more easily enjoy the spectacular features of our ocean shores.

Seaweeds, not the easiest plants to harvest, often grow in wet, slippery, inaccessible places, where labor is scarce. Their great bulk and short shelf life are deterring factors, and except in the Orient, farming, harvesting and preserving techniques exist in a primitive stage. Yet, considering their potential for contribution to better nutrition, as well as providing interest, variety and delectable taste, it seems remarkable that seaweeds are not better known and appreciated. Incredibly, many pay up to $40, or more, for a pound of dried, commercial algal preparations, when fresh seaweed is superior and free for the taking.

Resistance to change is perhaps one reason sea vegetables have not caught on in modern America. Moreover, the cast-up seaweeds encountered on a casual trip to the beach may not seem at all palatable. But if one views the fresh sea vegetables exposed at low tides, moving and supported by the nourishing ocean, it would be hard not to appreciate their beauty.

What Are Seaweeds?

Marine plants (seaweeds) fall into two main groups: the marine algae, the subject of this discussion, and marine grasses, which are descendants of "higher" seed-producing land plants. Algae, variously classified as belonging to at least eight major groups plus several subgroups, are quite diverse. Comprising more than 20,000 species, both fresh water and marine, they range in size from microscopic unicellular forms to giants which rival our coast redwoods in length. The larger benthic, or attached algae, commonly referred to as seaweeds, occur mostly in the intertidal and continental shelf areas, less than 8% of the ocean area. Since plants require sunlight for the photosynthetic manufacture of food, marine plants must remain in the upper levels of water (photic zone) where sunlight penetrates. They accomplish this by various means of flotation, or by attaching themselves to rocks and other structures in the shallower parts of the ocean. Many of these larger algae possess hollow, gas-filled floats which provide buoyancy.

Accounting for 95% of the vegetation of the sea, the free-floating, mostly microscopic algae phytoplankton, belong to several different plant groups. The nutrients produced by marine plants are in large part cycled through micro-organisms, bacteria and protozoa, which are then ingested by small marine animals at the "bottom" of the food "pyramid" or "web." These in turn are eaten by larger animals and finally by fish, birds and man at the "top" of the pyramid. In terms of their abundance, microscopic algae, called diatoms, dino- flagellates and other photosynthetic algae, are the most important of the planktonic plant forms. They drift in clouds in the sea providing grazing for copepods and krill, which in turn are fed upon by baleen whales and other sea animals. Under certain conditions, including influx of nutrient-rich waters, these clouds of phytoplankton burst into frantic fertility, resulting in a magnificent feast for higher marine life. Such a "bloom" may become so dense that pigments of its members color the sea. Blooms of one such dinoflagellate, *Gymnodinium breve*, breed death. At the peak of the deadly "red tide" bloom, concentrations of *Gymnodinium breve*, may reach 6 million cells per liter, coloring the water red. Among the wastes excreted are powerful toxins which affect the nervous system of fish, immobilizing their gills. The massive decomposition resulting from the killed fish fuels the bloom until the oxygen content of the water is exhausted, suffocating the fish that have not yet taken in the toxin. Such occurrences result in severe losses to the fishing and tourist industries, and annoyance to residents in areas where large numbers of dead fish wash onto the beaches and into the bays. Toxins of certain dinoflagellates belonging to *Gymnodinium* and *Gonyaulax* are concentrated by mussels, clams and other shellfish of the Pacific coast, making it necessary to discontinue their harvest in some areas during the summer months, which can be a time of heavy bloom. So far researchers have been unable to control such red tides, or to develop an antidote for the poisoning. Fortunately for the sea vegetable forager, sea vegetables are not affected by these toxins and may be safely used even during a "red tide" alert.

Seaweed Classification

The large marine algae (seaweeds or sea vegetables), fall into three main groups based on their chemical substances, food reserves and presumed relationships: Chlorophyta, or green algae; Rhodophyta, or red algae; and Phaeophyta, or brown algae. Though these names are based on the different colors of photosynthetic pigments in the green, red and brown groups, seaweeds are not readily classified by the apparent colors alone.

Sometimes grouped with the seaweeds are Cyanophyta, or blue-green algae. These primitive filamentous forms are sometimes classified with bacteria due to the similarity in cell structure. Certain rocks laid down three to four billion years ago contain impressions of the earth's first life – fossil algae which resemble modern blue-green algae. Blue-green algae, often microscopic or filamentous, lie loose or form an irregular or matted dark-blue to black layer. Few blue-green algae are of interest to seaweed collectors. There are tropical forms known as *Lyngbya* which can cause skin irritations, and others which are responsible for the poisonous nature of some reef-fish which feed on them. One toxic form, *Lyngbya aestuarii*, "mermaid's hair," sometimes occurs as a dark bluish-green filamentous mat on mudflats. Several fresh water members of blue-green algae, including *Spirulina* and *Nostoc*, are cultured and used as an extremely nutritious food supplement.

All marine algae contain the green pigment, chlorophyll, by which energy from the sun is used to manufacture energy-rich plant foods from inorganic substances, and carbon dioxide. In addition they often have yellow, red and orange pigments (xanthophylls and carotenes). Chlorophyta, or green algae, are bright green in color and are the ancestors of land plants. In this group are many of the familiar microscopic and macroscopic algae, both fresh water and marine. There are 7,000 species of Chlorophyta, only 13% of which are marine. The cells contain starch (the same as in higher plants) and typical cell organelles which aid in identification. They are found primarily in shallow water of 1.5 to 45 feet (0.5 to 15 meters) but some species occur in deeper water to 500 feet (150 meters).

In addition to chlorophyll, Rhodophyta, or red and blue-green algae, contain water soluble protein-bound pigments called phycobilins, which are red (c-phycoerythrin) or blue (c-phycocyanin). Rhodophyta range in color from all shades of red, green, and grey to almost black. Comprising of 4,000 species, all but 2% of which are marine, most red seaweeds flourish in tropical and subtropical regions. The food reserve, non-soluble carbohydrate, differs from that in green algae. Red seaweeds are harvested for the extracts agar and carrageenan, and for food.

The Phaeophyta, or brown algae, are the familiar kelps, some of which are extremely large. The green chlorophyll pigments, masked by golden or brown pigments called xanthophylls, create a brown to greenish-brown color. Including 1,500 species, almost all of which are marine, Phaeophyta flourish in cold temperate to arctic marine waters. Morphologically, the brown seaweeds are the most complex algae, with "stems" (stipes), "leaves" (blades or lamina), "'floats" or "bulbs" (bladders) and "roots" (haptera). The food reserves are laminarin, a carbohydrate, and mannitol, an alcohol. Some are harvested in great amounts for alginate (a gel). Once these algae were burned for the extraction of carbonate of soda, and used in the manufacture of glass and soap. The term "kelp," which was used for this product, has since been applied to any of the large brown seaweeds.

Seaweed Names

Many of our most promising sea vegetables have no widely recognized common names, and are called by the Latin names set down by marine botanists who first described the species. Generally those plants that do have common names, such as "dulse" (Palmaria palmata), giant Pacific kelp

(Macrocystis pyrifera), or "Turkish towel" *(Gigartina exasperata)* have been widely used for food or chemicals, or have some eye-catching feature.

Since common names such as nori, wakame, kelp or kombu have been applied to more than one alga, the correct Latin name is the best way to clearly designate a particular alga. The Latin name includes two italicized or underlined words, the genus and species. When referring to a very common alga such as "sea lettuce," the genus name *(Ulva)* is often used. To be more precise the two-word Latin name, *Ulva lactuca*, or *U. lactuca*, distinguishes a particular species of sea lettuce. The Latin name *"lactuca"* refers to a certain species of the genus *Ulva* (as distinguished from another similar plant such as *Ulva expansa*, for instance). The name of the author who first described the species will sometimes follow the species name – *Ulva lactuca* L. (for Linnaeus). Other common seaweeds such as the sea palm or bullwhip kelp are easily distinguished by their common names, or may be referred to merely by the generic name, *Postelsia* or *Nereocystis*, since there are no other West Coast species of these genera. There are several useful guides to seaweeds, with clear descriptions and good photographs or line drawings. No one small book will include all the seaweeds which occur, so having more than one book is helpful. The guides listed in the Bibliography by Scagel, Waaland, Abbott, Dawson, Lee, Gosner, and Hanson, are very useful especially for beginners. Older guides may use names which are no longer valid, but contain useful information and descriptions. These name changes often reflect new interpretations of complicated life cycles of algae and relationships to other algae. It often becomes a challenge for an amateur seaweed hunter to track down the correct names. But knowing the formal name and classification of a particular seaweed will indicate related species and thus serve as a tool in learning more about its properties.

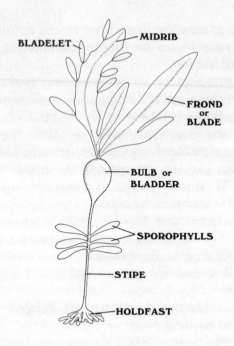

Structure of Seaweeds

Having evolved very early in the geological history of the earth, marine algae have changed very little from their early forms, though in some cases they are now more complex. Higher plants, which evolved from the algae, differ in having complicated structures for specific functions, such as roots which absorb nutrients, stems which conduct nutrients in solutions and provide support, and leaves which photosynthesize. Although the structure of algae resemble these organs, the entire plant has a very simple organization with the bulk serving both photosynthetic and reproductive functions. They produce no flowers, seeds or fruits, as in higher plants, but reproduce by a bewildering variety of alternations of single-celled and leafy forms, both asexual and sexual.

Seaweeds need no "woody" supporting or conductive

tissues, since they are buoyed up by the surrounding water which also provides a nourishing environment for exchange of dissolved substances, gases and essential minerals needed throughout the plant for its nutrition, growth and reproduction. The seaweed body or thallus, consists of some sort of holdfast which forms the attachment to the substrate (usually rock) and the main portion of the plant. The thallus may consist of simple flattened blades resembling leaves, or it may have a stem-like stipe supporting the blades. Some species have gas-filled floats. In some there is an obvious midrib down the middle of the blade. As in land plants, seaweeds have every conceivable form and texture. The thallus may be broad, narrow, leafy, tough, flat, tubular, encrusting, branched, or composed of fine filaments.

Reproduction of Algae

For bewildering variety and complexity, nothing beats the reproductive cycle of seaweeds. The reproductive cycle of most algae involves two distinct phases: a sexual, egg and sperm-producing stage (gametophyte generation); and an asexual, spore-producing stage (sporophyte generation). The reproductive cells are microscopic, and often borne in specialized structures on the thallus. In some of the simpler filamentous forms, asexual reproduction may occur by fragmentation of the plant. There is typically alternation of generations, the gametophyte stage producing gametes which fuse (fertilization) and the resulting embryo developing into a sporophyte stage. The sporophyte produces spores, each of which develops into a gametophyte, completing the cycle. However, there is tremendous variation, and in the red seaweeds, complex subcycles and two sporophyte stages. As in "higher" plants, the most conspicuous stage is usually the sporophyte, although in some such as Enteromorpha, the sporophyte and gametophyte generations look identical. For details of life cycles of algae see books by Waaland, Scagel, or Dawes listed in the Bibliography.

Where Seaweeds Grow

The depth at which seaweeds can survive and grow in the ocean is limited by the depth to which sunlight penetrates. In clear waters the longer, red to orange components of sunlight are absorbed in the upper layers, while the shorter, blue wavelengths penetrate to greater depths. Thus there is a tendency for red seaweeds which have pigments for using the shorter, blue light wavelengths to survive at the greatest depths, while brown seaweeds are intermediate, and green seaweeds are found nearest the surface. In clear waters seaweeds often grow down to depths of 150 feet (50 meters) or deeper. In exceptionally clear water in the tropics, certain red algae have been reported growing at depths of 600 feet (200 meters). But in more muddy and polluted waters, or in the plankton-rich murky waters of the Pacific Northwest, seaweed growth may stop only six to nine feet below low tide level.

Many species, never exposed to the atmosphere, can only be seen by wading, diving or dredging, or when torn loose and cast up on the shore by storms. But many marine algae can withstand varying degrees of exposure to the air and sun, and are found in specific levels of tidal exposure where we can view them during low tides.

Most seaweeds live attached to a solid substrate, usually rock. Concrete breakwaters, pilings and seawalls also support luxurient growth of marine animals and plants, as do wooden pilings and docks. Some seaweeds are epiphytic, that is, grow attached to other marine plants or animals. A few kinds, such as *Gracilaria* grow attached to rocks, shells or pebbles in sandy or muddy areas.

The Tides

The daily rise and fall of sea levels, due to the gravitational pull of the moon and sun, is the most important force affecting animal and plant life of coastal intertidal waters. On the Atlantic and Pacific coasts the tidal cycles are semidiurnal, meaning two high tides and two low tides occur daily. On the Atlantic side, the two highs and two lows are more or less equal, and the range of tidal extremes average three to four feet, with the famous exception of the greatest tides in the world found in the Bay of Funday, which average almost 45 feet at spring tides. On the Pacific coast, the semidiurnal tides consist of two highs and two lows of unequal height, and the greatest tidal ranges are found in the upper reaches of Puget Sound. Tides are greatest when the earth, sun and moon are lined up, near full moon and new moon. These extreme tides are called spring tides. On the other hand, when the moon is at right angles to the earth-sun line, near the first and last moon quarters, we have the less extreme, or neap tides. Each day the time at which high or low tide occurs is progressively later. In addition, the tide's magnitude is greatly affected by the shape of the shorelines and topography of the ocean bottom.

Some species of seaweeds are only uncovered during the lowest or "minus" spring tides. Since these tides only last a brief time, it would be wise to consult local tidal tables and plan your trips accordingly. During daylight hours, the best tides occur in the spring months.

Zonation

In the intertidal* area different factors of exposure result in zonation patterns, which are particularly noticeable on steep rock faces. Many chemical, physical, biological, and climatic factors play a part in determining which algae will occur at a particular tidal level, including length of exposure time, grazing by marine animals, shading, light intensity, temperature, rainfall, humidity, fog, salinity, dissolved oxygen, available nutrients, carbon dioxide, pollution, changes in pH, water movement, spray, surf, tides, upwelling, winds, and currents. Nevertheless, various algae species can usually be found at specific tide levels, and the terms, upper, mid, low, and subtidal, more or less characterize a world-wide zonal pattern.

* The term "littoral" is often used as a synonym for "intertidal," but littoral also includes the splash or spray zone (littoral fringe), above the upper tidal zone.

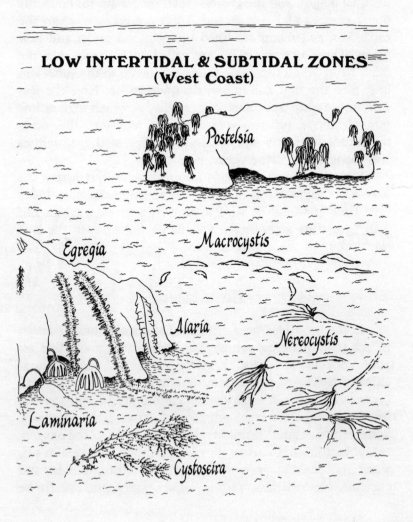

LOW INTERTIDAL & SUBTIDAL ZONES
(West Coast)

Postelsia

Egregia

Macrocystis

Alaria

Nereocystis

Laminaria

Cystoseira

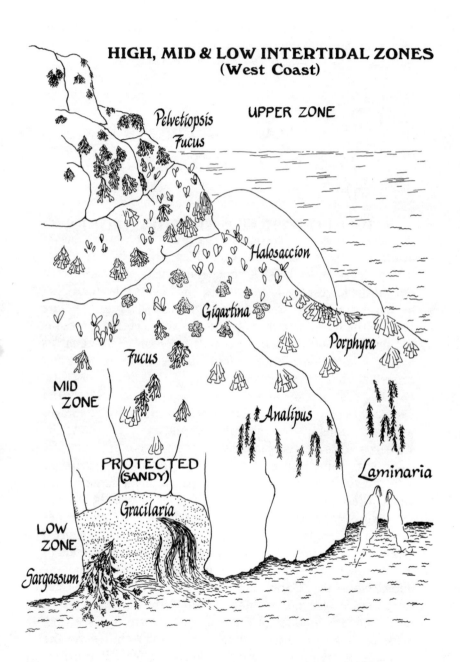

HIGH, MID & LOW INTERTIDAL ZONES
(West Coast)

UPPER ZONE

Pelvetiopsis
Fucus

Halosaccion

Gigartina

Porphyra

Fucus

MID
ZONE

Analipus

PROTECTED
(SANDY)

Laminaria

Gracilaria

LOW
ZONE

Sargassum

CHAPTER TWO
TIPS FOR THE FORAGER

"Tide's out, soup's on!" could be the song of the sea vegetable forager. The lower the tide, the more species available. While some sea vegetables occur in the upper intertidal levels, such as *Porphyra* and *Pelvetiopsis*, many exist only at the lowest levels and require the lowest tides for diving or harvesting. (See illustration, pages 32 - 33.) But, before visiting the rocky shores at low tide, it would be advantageous to first obtain a tide table specifically for your area. The tables based on U.S. Coast and Geodetic Survey are quite good and available from most sporting stores.

The spectacular rocky shores of the northern Atlantic and Pacific coasts of the United States provide the seaweed forager with an unparalleled abundance and variety of edible seaweeds. This cornucopia continues the length of the Pacific coast, with some changes in forms. On the northern Atlantic side the cold rough waters of the Arctic favor large brown kelps. These give way in turn to the green seaweeds, such as sea lettuce, south of Long Island Sound where sandy beaches and shallow bays predominate. Smaller reds and calcified green seaweeds prevail in the Florida Keys and coral reefs of the southern regions. Warm Gulf Stream waters, moving north from the Caribbean, influence the air and water temperature over the continental shelf. Cape Cod represents a north-south boundary for many species. North of Cape Cod, kelps such as *Laminaria*, flourish in waters chilled by the Labrador Current, while more tropical species fail north of Massachusetts Bay.

Top left, the author holding *Egregia* and *Alaria.* Right, husband Bayard with *Nereocystis* with attached *Porphyra nereocystis.* Bottom, author, husband Bayard, Prof. Ed Lippert and student with *Nereocystis* with attached *Porphyra nereocystis.*

What Seaweeds Can Be Used

Universally appreciated for qualities of flavor, texture and appearance, a number of especially favored sea vegetable species appear on the menus serving many coastal people. Many other species, not widely distributed, still enjoy local popularity. The West Coast of America favors an abundance of large, easy to harvest, especially tasty varieties, many of which do not occur in other regions. The algae forager may safely try any of the seaweeds (see note* below). Each species possesses its own individual flavor, color, texture and chemical composition, some highly prized, others less so. Some, such as species of *Laurencia*, sparingly used as a spice add a nice flavor to several dishes, while others are used as land vegetables are. One group, *Desmarestia*, contains dilute sulfuric acid and is therefore unpleasant to the taste, and would perhaps cause upset if eaten in quantity (see pp. 109 to 110). Others, such as the coralline algae, are encrusted with calcium compounds, and thus inedible. Algae that are abundant and known to be good, will be described and recipes given, but these certainly should not be considered the only ones to look for and experiment with.

Using the scientific names of marine algae is preferred, especially since common names don't exist or the same name for one seaweed may apply to another. It is true, sea vegetables, at first, may seem strange, the names difficult to pronounce, and the negative connotation of "weed" in their common name a "turn-off," but overriding these slight disadvantages is that the abundant choice of sea vegetables not only adds zest to all kinds of foods but nutritional quality as well.

Some of the common seaweeds in the U.S., including species of *Ahnfeltia, Gigartina, Ulva, Codium, Enteromorphya, Laurencia,* and *Scytosiphon,* are closely related to favorite sea vegtables in Hawaii and the Orient. *Palmaria palmata* (dulse), a great favorite of Atlantic coastal people, which is relatively rare on the West Coast, is included in the section on Commercial and Imported Seaweeds.

*Note: As mushroom foragers are aware, many plant groups contain members which are exceedingly toxic. Seaweeds, however, are relatively free of this danger. There is a filamentous blue-green alga, *Lyngbya*, of concern in the tropics (see Chapter I, What Are Seaweeds?). Chemical studies have been carried out recently on a number of seaweeds in order to determine the nature of physiologically active compounds which could have medical importance. A few types of seaweed contain substances which might give problems if consumed in great quantity. Species of *Desmarestia* contain sulfuric acid. Certain members of the *Laurencia* group contain a peppery tasting substance which may be toxic. *Caulerpa*, a tropical group cultivated for human consumption has some members which may be toxic for some individuals. Caulerpicin, responsible for the peppery taste of *C. lamourouxii*, causes a mild anesthesia when placed on the tongue. Potent chemicals of this group may be concentrated in the food chain. The tropical genus *Asparagopsis*, a favorite in Hawaii and Java, has toxic compounds which are removed by soaking before eating.

How To Harvest Seaweeds

In harvesting sea vegetables, take great care (observe local regulations; see pp. 212-215) to insure the survival and regrowth of plants, where possible. For instance, in harvesting *Pelvetiopsis*, scissors may be used to snip off the plants, leaving the holdfasts to ensure continued development. Since this holdfast is often encrusted with shell, it requires trimming before eating anyway. In the case of *Alaria*, the blade should be cut well above the sporophylls (the small oval reproductive blades at the base of the large blade) so that the plant can continue to grow and reproduce. Discard frayed ends and discolored portions. The long *Laminaria* species may be cut in the middle of the blade leaving the lower portion intact for further growth. The center portion of *Laminaria* (kelp) is considered the most nutritious and delicious part. *Nereocystis* (bull kelp), an annual, will not grow further when cut below the bulb. If only a portion of the *Nereocystis* fronds (leafy part) are taken, the remaining plant may continue to grow. At present, there is little concern about overharvest of this kelp, but in the case of *Postelsia* (sea palm), there is evidence of overharvest in California. With this in mind, leave small plants to grow, and enough whole plants intact to assure propagation. Cut off only part of the fronds, leaving three inches or so to continue growing and reproducing.

In short, do not gather rare species, or more than half the population of abundant species. Observe local regulations, and take great care not to disturb or trample plants and animals unnecessarily. Overharvesting of most West Coast sea vegetables is not yet a problem. Still, a considerate forager will only cut or clip portions of plants where possible. The spring and summer months, when growth rates are high, plants are tender, and low tides occur at daylight hours, attract sea vegetable collectors. Of course, common sense suggests gathering healthy fresh plants from unpolluted places.

Keep gathered seaweeds as cold as possible and separate from *Desmarestia,* as the high acid content of this particular species will destroy everything in the bucket. Buckets, or bags of net or plastic are handy for collecting and storing. Fresh sea vegetables keep better if drained of water and stored at low temperatures.

How To Use Sea Vegetables

Sea vegetables, amazingly simple to use, require, at most, a brief washing and picking over. Prolonged soaking in fresh water should be avoided to preserve flavor and vitamins. Most become quite tender with very little cooking. *Porphyra* may be tenderized with shoyu (tamari or soy sauce). Soups and stir fries are the simplest recipes to start with, and most seaweeds can be used this way. It is also possible to include a sea vegetable in almost any dish for added nutrition, plus interesting and pleasing appearance. Their flavors blend with many popular seasonings and regional cooking methods. They can be sautéed, boiled, baked, steamed, blanched, or fried, and preserved by drying, pickling, salting, freezing, canning or candying. There are endless possibilities for discovery, innovation and creation.

Some people use sea vegetables raw, but more commonly

they are served cooked and seasoned. Some species of *Gigartina, Ahnfeltia, Gelidium* and *Gracilaria* are used to thicken puddings, candies and other desserts. (The interested cook may consult Judith Madlener's two sea vegetable books: see Bibliography.) Prolific algae, including *Hedophyllum* and the many species of *Iridaea*, offer little reward to the sea vegetable forager, becoming quite gummy and/or unappetizing in flavor when cooked. Abundant algae such as the large kelps serve as fertilizer, animal fodder, and as sources of pharmaceuticals, chemicals and colloids, important in a number of industries.

Preserving Sea Vegetables

Sea vegetables are tastier when fresh, but many have limited keeping qualities. Drying is the usual method of preservation, though some can be successfully frozen.

Many seaweeds preserve well dried outside, requiring a day in sunny weather. If not completely dried at the end of the day, they should be taken inside, and with a fan the drying process can be finished, or it can be completed outside the next day. When completely dry, some seaweeds become very brittle and should be allowed to relax or become pliable. This can be accomplished by placing the seaweed in a cool shady place for a short time before packing. When stored in tight jars, cans, or double plastic bags, dried seaweeds will keep for a year or longer. In commercial packaging a desiccant may be included, such as a bag of silica gel. When reconstituted by soaking in water, they may appear almost like fresh seaweeds.

Some of the choicest sea vegetables, including *Pelvetiopsis* and *Nereocystis* are best eaten in the fresh state. *Pelvetiopsis*, however, will keep fairly well in the refrigerator and *Nereocystis* may be pickled. Some fresh sea vegetables, such as *Alaria*, spoil very quickly but may be dried or frozen. After soaking in water, dried *Alaria* closely resembles the fresh sea vegetable. Many sea vegetables are known to most people

Sea vegetable solar drying house.

Drying seaweed outdoors.

only in the dry state. Dried dulse *(Palmaria palmata)* for example, has been enjoyed for centuries as a snack. In Japan a number of sea vegetable species appear in the market in various dried forms, including hijiki *(Hizikia)*, wakame *(Undaria)*, nori *(Porphyra)* and kombu *(Laminaria)*. Another seaweed used by the Japanese, *Analipus japonicus* (matsumo) is often preserved in soy sauce with mushrooms, but our West Coast foragers may enjoy fresh fir needle (the western common name for *Analipus)*. For many species of sea vegetables, foragers will have to experiment to learn which methods of preparation and preservation to use.

Tips From the Professionals

We are indebted to professional harvesters, Matthew Hodel of California; Shepard and Linnette Erhart of Franklin, Maine; and Larch and Jan Hansen of Steuben, Maine; for sharing their experiences and information. (See p. 229 for addresses of suppliers. Also see book by Lewallen listed in the Bibliography.)

Professional harvesters use equipment ranging from sneakers and boots, to wet suits and boats. Seaweed (unrinsed in fresh water) is dried, sometimes outside in good weather, or inside, using heat and fans. (In Oregon, I have found that most seaweeds collected close to shore should be rinsed with fresh water to free it of sand and clinging invertebrates.)

In the cold waters of the northern Atlantic and Pacific Oceans, seaweeds grow the fastest during the spring and summer months, though harvesting may continue into autumn and winter. Matthew Hodel leases tidelands from the State of California for his collecting. To gather sea vegetables he uses a boat and wet suit. To preserve the seaweed, he dries them unrinsed, in buildings using heat and fans. *Alaria, Laminaria, Postelsia, Nereocystis* (both dried fronds and pickles made from the stipe), and *Porphyra nereocystis* (red nori) is then marketed.

On the East Coast, according to Larch and Jan Hansen, *Palmaria palmata* (dulse) often imported from Canada, accounts for half the sea vegetable sales. This is followed by *Laminaria longicruris* (kelp/kombu), *Alaria esculenta, L. digitata* (horsetail kelp), *Chondrus crispus* (Irish moss), and *Porphyra umbilicalis* (nori). No license for harvesting is required at present, though a fee is paid for production.

Gathered into bushel baskets by hand, dulse is collected at low tide. Wearing hip boots is helpful, and gloves, late in the season, are needed for warmth. Dulse is dried on net-covered racks either in the sun, or in heated sheds. The season for dulse on the East Coast is June-August, although there can be good picking as late as November.

Boots or a boat are needed for kelp/kombu harvest. The season for *L. longicruris* extends from March to May, although it can also be found in winter. Young plants are crisp; older ones large, soft and sweet with mannitol. This sea vegetable is hung up to dry from high poles. *L. digitatais* is said to be richer and sweeter than *L. longicruris.*

The young (small) tender blades of *Alaria esculenta* are a favorite East Coast sea vegetable, but most difficult to find. Since it grows in deep, cold, highly agitated waters on rocky, wave-swept points, and storms sweep the coast during May and June when young *Alaria* is prime, harvesting is quite challenging. Later in the season, larger blades are collected, which require longer cooking.

In western coastal waters the *Alaria* species seem tender and choice throughout the growing season. Professional harvester Matthew Hodel leaves the sporophylls for further reproduction, and reports that *Alaria* stands may be cropped at least four times during the growing season.

Summary of Essentials for Foraging and Storage of Sea Vegetables

Harvest at a "minus" low tide, unless you plan to swim, snorkel or grapple sea vegetables from a boat. Begin as the tide is still going out, or before it turns. Consult the tide tables for your locality for information.

Have the right equipment. Wear appropriate clothing for your climate. Wear wool, or a wet suit for prolonged exposure to cold weather. Wading boots, or heavy shoes or sneakers with corrugated soles help grip the slippery rocks. Sunburn protection (hat with brim, lotions) may also be necessary. Have a knife, scissors, or linoleum knife for cutting sea vegetables. Sufficient containers for carrying off the bounty are plastic bags (punch holes for draining), buckets, clothes baskets, porous bags such as onion bags, pillowcases, or back packs. Canvas bags with drawstrings which may be fastened to the belt if wading or swimming are also good. Use an ice chest, heavy blanket or sleeping bag to insulate seaweed from heat while in transit. Have bucket pans or large drums for washing, and colanders for draining seaweeds. Nets bags may be useful for washing small sea vegetables. Screens or lines for drying are necessary; or dry small quantities in a food drier.

To take care of the sea vegetables collected, keep the plants cool. Separate from *Desmarestia*. Store fresh plants in the refrigerator. Wash quickly in cool fresh water to get rid of sand and shells. Dry by hanging large seaweeds from lines, and spreading smaller ones on toxic free screens, netting or cloth in the sun and breeze until thoroughly dry. Alternative methods of drying are: spreading in front of a fire or over the stove, if not too hot, or using a food dryer. Store the dried vegetables in air-tight containers away from heat, sunlight and dampness. Double or triple plastic bags work well.

CHAPTER THREE
NUTRITION FROM THE SEA

Composition
& Nutritive Values of Seaweeds

In their living, natural state, seaweeds are composed of from 80 to 90% water; dried, they contain 10 to 20% water. They average about 50% carbohydrates, include high percentages of minerals (7 to 38%) and have abundant vitamins. Raw protein content ranges from around 7% in *Laminaria* (kelp or kombu), to 35% or more in some *Porphyra* species (nori). They generally contain only one to two percent fat.

Seaweeds have remarkable cellular components which enable them to withstand the rigors of their saline environment. Some of the carbohydrates of sea vegetables are polysaccharides with properties quite different from those of land plants. Although it was assumed that some of these are indigestible and thus could not contribute directly to human nutrition, it has been observed that persons whose diet includes sea vegetables do obtain good nutrition and energy from them.

Sadly, little research has been conducted to determine composition of U.S. sea vegetables and their utilization in human nutrition. Recent research in Japan has shown that their most popular sea vegetable, *Porphyra* (nori) has a very high digestibility of 70% for carbohydrates and high quality protein. Sea vegetables in past times have have been very important to the nutritional health and cultures of coastal peoples. For detailed information on the chemical composition of sea vegetables see *Vegetables From The Sea* by Seibin and Teruko Arasaki.

The extraordinarily high vitamin and mineral content of sea vegetables is their most obvious health benefit. The vitamin content for each species varies with the season, environmental condition, and of course, freshness or method of preservation. Sea vegetables have more of such vitamins as A, B_1, B_2, B_5, B_{12}, and C; pantothenic acid, folic acid, and niacin, than fresh fruits and land vegetables.

In the form of beta-carotene, Vitamin A is extraordinarily high in the sea vegetables nori *(Porphyra)*, and dulse *(Palmaria palmata)*. Nori dried in sheets contains as much as 50,000 IU's of vitamin A per 100 grams.

The vitamin C content of seaweeds is high. In dulse, nori and *Alaria* it is said to be one and a half times more than in oranges. In tested Norwegian seaweed meal, the vitamin C ranged from 500 to 2000 mg. per kilogram. The daily requirement of vitamin C of 50 to 60 mg. would be available in about one ounce (2.8 grams) of meal.

Kombu *(Laminaria)* rivals red meat and milk products in B vitamins. Marine algae are often very rich in vitamin B_{12} and thus are one of the few plant sources of this vitamin, containing more than many animal organs. Although occurrence of vitamin B_{12} is quite general, as a rule brown algae are lowest, red algae next, and green algae highest. It has been found that bacteria living epiphytically on the seaweeds are the primary source of vitamin B_{12}.

Algae contain steroids, precursors of vitamin D, which are converted into vitamin D in the body. Also sea vegetables contain significant amounts of vitamin E and K.

As can be seen in the nutritional tables, there is some discrepancy in the values for a given sea vegetable and considerable differences between sea vegetable species. Since the usual portion of sea vegetables is small (around .5 ounce, or 14.5 grams), the contribution of sea vegetables to the total daily requirement of many vitamins and protein in most diets would be rather minimal.

Seasonal variation in vitamin content is great; for example, in the *Alaria* species analyzed, vitamin B_{12} increases five-fold from February to May, then decreases to half as much by August. Folic acid content varies in a similar way with season and species. No simple harvest time rule can be given for gathering algae with high vitamin content. The concentration of some vitamins show maxima in spring and summer (e.g. vitamin B_{12} and folic acid), whereas other vitamins have their concentration maxima in the winter (e.g. niacin and folinic acid). Niacin and pantothenic acid contents also vary among algae, being quite high for *Alaria*. The content of vitamin B_{12}, folic acid, folinic acid and pantothenic acid and vitamin B_1 is generally higher in the green and red algae than in the brown. The niacin and vitamin C content are similar for red, brown and green algae.

The gluey substance in red algae, called galactose, is extractable with hot water, forming various viscid polysaccharides, which form the basis for many important commercial products. There are three main types of gelatinous substances obtained from red seaweeds with different properties and uses: agar, carrageenan and funoran. Hot water extracts of these polysaccharides produce a viscous liquid, which upon cooling, gels. The gelatin power of agar is strong, whereas that of funoran and carrageenan is weak.

The origins of seaweed extracts for Japanese culinary delicacies date from over 1200 years ago when *Gelidium* species were boiled to prepare a dish called tokoroten. The story is told of the accidental discovery of agar in the late 17th century, when left-over tokoroten was thrown out and became frozen during the cold winter night. A few days later someone discovered that the resultant spongy, white, dry material, when added to water and boiled, would re-congeal into a delicacy more pure and delicious than the original. A local inn started serving it, and a famous priest gave it the name, kanten, by which this type of agar is known today.

Carrageenan is the mucilaginous substance of red algae in the Gigartinacea family, including *Chondrus crispus* (Irish moss), and *Gigartina stellata*. Dried *Chondrus crispus* is boiled by the coastal people of Ireland and mixed with milk. The name of the gel, carrageenan, came from the village Carragheen, where Irish moss to this day is gathered and distributed. It is used widely in folk medicine as treatment for respiratory disease. It also has many commercial and industrial uses.

Algin, or alginic acid, is the mucilage material found in many brown algae. Though not itself utilized in human nutrition, plenty of calories are consumed along with algin, which is used as a thickener and stabilizer in ice cream, beer and other goodies. It also has its uses in products used to promote weight loss. It has many uses in medicine and is used in a number of industries.

Sorbitol, a sweet-tasting sugar alcohol occurring in some red algae, is used widely for diet and diabetes patients as a sugar substitute. Mannitol, the sugar alcohol which occurs in brown algae, has a sweetness of about 60% that of sucrose. It is often found as a white powder on the surface of kelp (*Laminaria*).

Recent information indicates that many sea vegetables furnish highly digestible, complete protein; that is, they have all the essential amino acids and thus are one of the few vegetable sources which supply complete protein. (However, dulse, *Palmaria palmata*, which is very high in protein, lacks the essential amino acid, tryptophane.) Soluble nitrogen compounds provide organic nitrogen in addition to the regular protein content. As with other elements in sea vegetables the level of protein depends on the species, season, place where it grows, age of plant, and etc. In the brown sea vegetables the highest amount of protein is found about two-thirds up in the frond. Seaweeds average around 9% protein, but some species are very high; e.g. *Enteromorpha intestinalis*, 20%; *Analipus japonicus*, 22%; *Gracilaria verrucosa*, 29%; and species of

Porphyra, 30% or more. *Porphyra* is therefore higher than soybeans and better than many meats in protein value.

Nitrogen content of sea vegetables ranges from 1.5 to 7.6% dry weight. When raw protein is calculated by multiplying nitrogen content by 6.5, the protein content ranges between 10 and 48%. The amino acid composition of proteins from the Japanese seaweeds tested by Arasaki is more favorable for human nutrition than that of land plants, and is similar to egg white, the standard used for human require- ments. Animal experiments and artificial digestion tests indicate that the Japanese favorites are highly nutritious. The non-protein nitrogen originates from amino acids, peptides, amines and nucleotides. Around 30 amino acids have been isolated in seaweeds, several of which are peculiar to them. In *Porphyra tenera* (nori), the amino acid alanine amounts to 25% of the free amino acids and accounts for the sweet taste. Isolated peptides include glutamic acid and aspartic acid in extracts from *Laminaria.*

Fat content of seaweed is low, approximately one to two percent of the dry weight, though rock weeds such as *Fucus* may run up to about eight percent. These differ from land plant oils in having more unsaturated than saturated fatty acids.

Sea vegetables contain more minerals than any other kind of food, not only all the minerals available in ocean water, but also many of the trace elements lacking in many areas of the world. Their surface tissues selectively absorb minerals from seawater, which account for from 7 to 38% of their dry weight. All the minerals required by human beings, including calcium, sodium, magnesium, potassium, phosphorus, iodine, iron, and zinc are present in significant amounts, plus many trace elements. Deficiency diseases caused by lack of various elements are widespread among farm animals, and presumably humans. Minerals which may be entirely leached out of soils are available to sea vegetables and concentrated by various seaweeds to a fantastic amount. Although we haven't exact nutritional information on American sea vegetables, some idea of the nutrition, vitamins and minerals can be obtained from analyses done elsewhere using related seaweeds.

Iodine is concentrated by many sea vegetables to a very high amount. In some it can be up to 40,000 times the amount in sea water. Potassium is concentrated 20 to 30 times the amount in sea water, while sodium is diluted greatly compared to sea water.

The iron content in seaweeds averages about 590 mg/kg of dry material. In a study of 59 species the minimum iron was 52 mg/kg and the maximum was 3,410 mg/kg. Daily human requirement of 10 to 18 mg iron is available in as little as 20 to 30 grams fresh weight of average seaweed. The uptake is enhanced by vitamin C, which can also be very high in seaweeds. The iron content of sea vegetables is from two to ten times that of egg yolks and spinach. According to Arasaki, the dried Japanese sea vegetables analyzed had the following iron content based on mg/100 grams: *Enteromorphya*, 106; *Ulva*, (sea lettuce) 87; *Hizikia*, (hijiki) 29; *Porphyra tenera*, (nori) 23; *Laminaria*, 15; *Undaria*, (wakame) 13; *Eisenia*, (arame) 12; *Analipus*, (matsumo, or fir needle) 10.

Some seaweeds are very high in calcium. Coralline algae concentrate calcium salts to form an exterior skeleton of lime, but of course these are not palatable. According to Arasaki, the calcium content in some sea vegetables tested ranged from (in mg/100g) 1,400 in *Hizikia fusiforme* (hijiki), 1,300 in *Undaria pinnatifida* (wakame), 1,170 in *Eisenia bicyclis* (arame), 890 in *Analipus japonicus* (matsumo or fir needle), 800 in *Laminaria* species, 730 in *Ulva* (sea lettuce) species, 600 in *Entromorpha* species, and 470 in *Porphyra tenera* (nori). The recommended daily allowance of 800 mg (1200 mg in teenagers) could be met in around 100 grams (3.5 ounces of most sea vegetables). It is not known if the calcium in sea vegetables is nutritionally effective, but if so, they could be one of the richest food source in this element. *Alaria* is also known to be very high in calcium. Calcium availability is higher in *Porphyra* than *Analipus*.

Brown algae are very high in iodine. The Chinese for

centuries have treated goiter caused by an iodine deficiency by means of iodine obtained from *Laminaria* (kombu) found in the waters around Japan. Now they are able to grow their own. One gram of kombu daily would provide the 0.1 to 0.2 milligrams required by a normal adult.

Research available indicates the following additional information on minerals in seaweeds: *Laminaria japonica* is high in potassium, *Analipus japonicus, Alaria crassifolia* and *Porphyra yezoensis* are fairly high in phosphorus; *Momostroma latissimum, Sytosiphon lomentaria* and *Codium fragile* are very high in iron and *Alaria* and *Porphyra* moderately high. *Gracilaria verrucosa* is extremely high in manganese. The availability of nitrogen, phosphorus and magnesium is very high in both *Monostroma* and *Gracilaria.* Generally the brown sea vegetables are richer in the major mineral elements than the green and red, especially in calcium and potassium. The green sea vegetables are high in magnesium and iron. Red algae are relatively poorer in both major and minor elements. Sea vegetables which are high in iron are also high in aluminum, titanium, chromium, manganese, cobalt and nickel, but not necessarily copper. The ratio of potassium to sodium in sea vegetables ranges from 3:2 to 3:1, possibly making kelp salts useful as salt substitutes in reducing sodium intake. In the past, North American Indians did not use salt, but substituted plant preparations, believing salt would make them prematurely gray like the white man and bring early death.

Unfortunately, it is not possible to give precise nutritional information including exact quantities of vitamins, minerals, etc. for each sea vegetable. Optimum human nutrition requires the supply of numerous dietary factors including at least 17 inorganic elements, various vitamins and essential amino acids. We are a long way from complete understanding of these factors in most foods, and experimental analyses of species of West Coast algae is very limited. Moreover, different researchers do not always agree on the nutritional contents of foods, and algae may vary in nutritional qualities depending on where it was grown.

Although we can't give as much information on the nutritional values of American sea vegetables as we would like, it can be assumed that they are among the most nutritious plants on earth. Dulse, a popular food item and folk remedy in ancient Iceland and Eighteenth Century England, has been widely used in British Columbia and exported to the U.S. It is still gathered and used as a relish by Indians of the Pacific Northwest, or cooked with other foods. The Native Americans continue to make considerable use of local species of *Porphyra*. Their use of seaweeds as food is believed to be responsible for the low incidence of goiter.

Are Seaweeds Safe From Pollution?

Coastal waters are rich in organic nutrients washed from agricultural and population centers. Although sewage may stimulate rich production of healthy plants, industrial wastes often prove harmful to marine algae. The seaweed industry of Japan has been plagued by pollution problems, causing them to move operations to less contaminated areas. Fuel oil has a distinctly harmful effect and has ruined seaweed harvests on many shores. Once, due to a combination of problems, including sewage, sea urchin cropping, and the near extermination of sea urchin-chomping sea otters, the important kelp industry of California was brought to near extinction. Through the heroic efforts of marine botanist Dr. Wheeler North and others, inter-relationships were understood, balance was restored, and the kelp beds were saved.

Seaweeds select and concentrate minerals important to nutrition in a fantastic amount. However, there is some evidence that harmful elements may also be concentrated, if present. For example, arsenic in nori has been shown to be higher in areas contaminated by industrial effluents. Other adverse growth effects on *Porphyra* have been caused by wastes from pulp mills, distilleries, and etc.

Certain seaweeds have a high ability to accumulate radio-active substances and thus are sensitive detectors for measuring radioactive contamination in surrounding waters. Useful scientific information has been gained by following radioactive or "labeled" compounds in the food chain. Although this property provides warning of fallout from atomic testing or nuclear disasters, it also may give cause to consider more carefully the area where we collect seafoods.

There have been numerous incidents of seaweed contamination in the Irish Sea off the coast of England from nuclear waste discharge by the Windscale Nuclear processing plant since it began operation 25 years ago. In spite of supervision and efforts to modify the process, the continuing hazard has resulted in hundreds of cases of leukemia and thyroid cancer in humans and deformities among livestock in the surrounding area. News reports of the accumulation of radioactive substances in *Porphyra* cultures in Japan from an unannounced nuclear accident caused a great uproar, since *Porphyra* culture is Japan's single most important marine resource. Presumably with the high standards under which this industry operates in Japan, contaminated seaweed would not be marketed. Apparently as yet there is no general hazard from radioactive strontium in sea water.

In spite of these considerations sea vegetables can still be relied on as pure, wholesome foods. The sticky mucilages found on the surfaces of most species are constantly being dissolved and washed off by the surrounding water, removing sand, silt and other impurities from the renewed surface. They are fresh, growing plants, bathed by the nourishing sea, and not sprayed with insecticides and pesticides as are so many land vegetables. Seaweeds serve as an important food base for a variety of marine animals. Those that look particularly nibbled on may not be considered prime for marketing, but would be no less wholesome than an unsprayed but wormy apple. Constant vigilance against needless pollution from oil drilling and transport, and toxic and radioactive waste dumping will be a permanent task for environmentalists of all countries for the survival of life on Earth.

CHAPTER FOUR

SEA VEGETABLES WITH SOYFOODS
For A Hungry Planet

The several causes and solutions to world hunger are beyond the scope of this book. However, a link in solving the enormous problem of world hunger is to increase regional food self-sufficiency. Gathering sea vegetables and combining them with high protein soyfoods can contribute to this kind of self-sufficiency, and contribute greatly to the health of populations.

Proteins, which make up about half of our body's framework of blood, bone, hair, muscles, skin, cartilage and tendons, as we all know, are vital for all the basic chemical reactions of life. Amino acids, the building blocks of proteins, are required in proper proportions in synthesizing the many proteins of our bodies, including hormones, enzymes, antibodies, and that all-important distribution and regulation system, the blood. The question is, how much protein do we need, and in what form? It is now recognized that the high quality proteins of meat, milk and eggs are not required for good human nutrition, and many Americans would be better off without the saturated fats and cholesterol these foods provide. Most plant foods contain the same essential amino acids as animal foods, but must be taken in proper combinations in order to achieve the optimum ratio of these amino acids.

It requires more than fourteen pounds of feedlot fodder protein to produce one pound of beef protein. A small increase in the demand for meat leads to an enormous decrease in the amount of grain and soy products available for human consumption. The poor are thus increasingly priced out of these high energy, high protein foods. An acre of land in beef production yields only about 20 pounds of useable protein. In soybeans, an acre yields up to 400 pounds, while an acre of suitable tidelands in cultured nori may yield up to 800 pounds useable protein. *Spirulina*, a blue-green alga, yields a fantastic 21,000 pounds of protein per acre when cultured.

For thousands of years people in the Orient have relied on soyfoods and sea vegetables as a means of providing good nutrition for their burgeoning populations. Tempeh and tofu, included in many of the following recipes, are two delicious and easily digested foods made from soybeans by processes which require low technology and energy. The soybean, a remarkable legume, and a complete protein similar to animal protein, contains all the amino acids essential to human nutrition. Served baked, boiled or roasted, only a portion of the food value is available, but transformed into tofu or tempeh, the digestibility and nutritional values are greatly enhanced. These delicious foods can serve as the backbone of a meatless diet for westerners as they have in East Asian countries. By using soy products in combination with grains and sea vegetables the proteins are complemented and the total utilizable protein boosted.

A number of widespread human diseases could easily be prevented, relieved or cured by the use of seaweeds or seaweed products. Goiter, the result of iodine deficiency, can cause severe mental and physical retardation; yet simple goiter is the easiest of all diseases to prevent. Most sea vegetables are very high in iodine, essential to thyroid function, and several seaweeds contain thyroxin, the hormone produced by the thyroid. Statistics show that there are 300 million people affected by goiter, mostly in areas where rain, flooding or glaciation has washed out the soil iodine. Ironically some of these areas are close to coasts rich in non-utilized algae.

Malnutrition in the poorer areas of the world is the root of many problems. Seaweeds, rich in vitamins, minerals, proteins, and trace elements could be used for the benefit of these populations, rather than exported for extractives; although protein deficiency will not be completely solved by the addition of seaweeds alone. Besides availability and cost, the amino acid ratio of some species may not be as favorable to human nutrition as are proteins from other sources. However, the very popular seaweed, nori *(Porphyra)* does have a favorable amino acid ratio and is very high in protein.

The books by Lappé and Collins, and Shurtleff and Ayoyagi listed in the Bibliography contain insightful discussions of the world hunger problem. These and several other delightful recipe books written by seaweed enthusiasts explain the uses and nutritive values of soyfoods, including *Tofu Madness* published by Island Spring Inc. and complied by Nancy Olszewski, *The Soy of Cooking* by Reggi Norton and Martha Wagner, and *The Sea Green Primer* by Juel Anderson and Richard Ford.

Per Acre Yield of Usable Protein From Different Food Sources

Porphyra, 750 lbs./acre
Spirulina, 21,000 lbs./acre

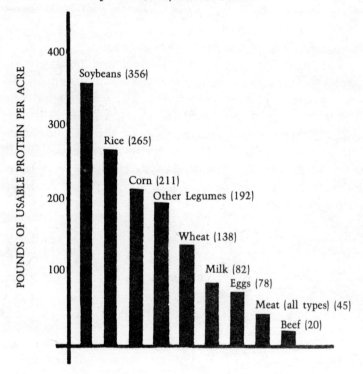

Per Acre Yields of Usable Protein (Reprinted with permission from *The Book of Tofu* by Shurtleff & Aoyagi, Ballantine Books, 1979.)

Table 2

High-Quality Protein
Food Comparison

Food	% Protein	Protein Quality (NPU %)	Current Price	Cost of One Day's Supply Usable Protein	Reference Used For Computations
Porphyra; nori (foraged)	35	?	Free!	Free!	150 grams/4.8 oz.
nori (imported)	35	?	$2.43/25g	$14	150 grams/4.8 oz.
soybeans	40	61	40¢/lb.	17¢ - 20¢	Shurtleff (Lappé)
tempeh, soy (homemade)	20	56	39¢/pound	29¢	Shurtleff & Aoyagi
soy grits	40	40	65¢/pound	31¢	Lappé
oatmeal	15	64	31¢/pound	31¢	Lappé
eggs	13	94	93¢/dozen	49¢	Lappé
tofu (homemade)	8	65	29¢/pound	56¢	Shurtleff & Aoyagi
buttermilk	4	81	50¢/quart	76¢	Lappé
hamburger	13	67	$1.45/pound	$1.17	Lappé
steak	20	67	$3.65/pound	$3.86	Lappé
tofu (commercial)	8	65	$1.00/pound	$1.70	Shurleff & Aoyagi
tempeh, soy (commercial)	20	56	$1.92/pound	$1.49	Shurtleff & Aoyagi
Spirulina (bulk)	60-65	57	$2.35/oz	$7.05/90g or 3oz.	Switzer

Note: NPU (Net Protein Utilization) is the measure of the amount of protein available for human nutrition. The above is not to suggest that anyone could or should rely on just one food for daily protein. Also, the cost of one day's supply of useable protein from algae may not take into account the NPU%, which would increase the amount needed.

Table 3

Nutritional Analysis of Four U.S. Sea Vegetables

100 gram sample analysis

	Protein-gms.	Fat-gms.	Carbohydrates-gms.	Fiber-gms.	Ash-gms.	Ca-mgs	K-mgs.	Na-gms.	Mg-mgs.	P-mgs.	Fe-mgs.	I-mgs.	Vit. A-IU	Vit. B-1	Vit. B-2	Vit. B-12	Niacin-mgs.	Vit C-summer mgs.
Kelp	7.3	1.1	55.0	3.0	22	800	5300	3.0	760	240	100	150	430	.08	.32	50	5.7	15
Alaria	12.7	1.5	48.0	3.6	18	1300	—	1.1	—	260	13	13	140	.11	.14	60	10.0	29
Dulse	25.3	3.2	44.0	1.3	22	567	8100	2.1	220	270	150	8	—	—	—	—	—	49
Nori	35.6	0.7	44.3	4.7	8	260	510	.6	—	—	12	—	11000	.25	1.24	—	10.0	20

Sources for chart: U.S. Dept. of Agriculture; Japan Nutritionist Association; *Composition and Facts About Foods*, Ford Heritage Health Research, Mokelumne Hill, CA 95245, 1698; *Seaweeds and Their Uses*, V. J. Chapman, Methuen & Co., Ltd, London 1950; "Kelp," Roseann C. Hirsch, *Bestways*; "Food From the Sea," Mary Schooner, *EastWest Journal*, Vol. 1, No. 6.

Table 4

Vitamin, Mineral & Protein Content Comparison

Sea Vegetables Versus Some Common Foods

Unit RDA, Adult	A IU 4 - 5,000	B₁ thiamin mg 1 - 1.5	B₂ riboflavin mg 1.1 - 1.6
Porphyra tenera, nori			
high quality.....................	**44,500**	**.25**	**1.24**
	6,357	.04	.18
med. quality.....................	**38,400**	**.21**	**1.00**
	5,485	.03	.14
low quality......................	**20,400**	**.12**	**.89**
	2,914	.02	.13
Ulva sp., sea lettuce	**960**	**.06**	**.03**
	137	.01	.004
Enteromorpha sp................	**500**	**.04**	**.52**
	71	.006	.07
Laminaria sp., kombu	**430**	**.08**	**.32**
	61	.01	.05
Hizikia fusiforme, hijiki	**150**	**.01**	**.20**
	21	.001	.03
Undaria pinnatifida, wakame	**140**	**.11**	**10.00**
	20	.02	1.40
Eisenia bicyclis, arame...........	**50**	**.02**	**.02**
	7	.004	.004
Whole wheat flour			
5/6 cup (100g, 3.5 oz.)	0	.55	.11
Spinach, 1 cup raw			
(55g, 1.8 oz.)......................	4,460	.06	.11
Milk, 1 cup whole			
(244g, 8.5 oz.)....................	310	.09	.40
Egg (without shell)			
(50g, 4 oz.).......................	260	.04	.15

* Vitamin A in sea vegetables is in the form of beta-carotene. Six micrograms beta-carotene = 1 microgram retinol; IU's are calculated on basis of retinol

Key: Bold no. = per 100 g (3.5 oz.) dry seaweed; light no. = average portion, 14.5g (0.5 oz.), about 1 cup packed, for *Porphyra*, and *Alaria*; and about 3 T *Hizikia* and *Porphyra tenera* (nori). Common food portions as indicated.

Niacin	C	B₅ pryridoxine	B₁₂	Calcium	Iron	Protein (raw)
mg	mg	mg	mg	mg	mg	g
13 - 18	50	2	3	800	10 - 18	44 - 66
10.00	**20.00**					
1.42	3.00					
3.00	**20.00**	**1.04**	**13-29**	**470**	**23.0**	**34.0**
.43	3.00	.15	2-4	64	3.0	5.0
2.60	**20.00**					
.37	3.00					
8.00	**10.00**		**6.30**	**730**	**87.0**	**15-24**
1.40	1.40		.09	104	12.4	2-3
1.00	**10.00**		**1.30**	**600**	**106.0**	**20.0**
.14	1.40		.19	85	15.0	3.0
1.80	**11.00**	**.27**	**.30**	**800**	**15.0**	**6-7**
.26	1.57	.04	.04	114	2.0	1.0
4.00	**0.00**		**.57**	**1400**	**29.0**	**6-8**
.57			.08	200	4.0	1.0
10.00	**15.00**			**1300**	**13.0**	**12.0**
1.40	2.14			185	1.9	1.7
2.60	**0.00**			**1170**	**12.0**	**7.5**
.37				167	2.0	1.0
4.30	0.00	.34	0.00	42	3.3	13.3
.30	28.00	.16	0.00	51	1.7	2.0
.20	2.00	.10	1.00	291	.1	8.0
trace	0.00	.06	1.00	28	1.0	6.0

equivalence. For humans, 1 retinol equivalent = 1 microgram retinol, or 6 micrograms beta-carotene.

Table 5

Mineral Analysis of Some Edible Japanese Seaweeds

Expressed on a dry weight basis.

		Monostroma latissimum	Analipus japonicus	Alaria crassifolia	Undaria pinnatifida	Laminaria angustata	Laminaria japonica	Laminaria religiosa	Porphyra yezoensis	Gracilaria verrucosa
Nitrogen	g%	1.40	3.48	3.35	1.56	1.55	1.49	1.94	5.35	4.61
Crude protein	g%	8.76	21.75	19.05	9.74	9.71	9.32	12.12	33.45	28.79
Sulfur	g%	6.27	2.33	0.80	1.00	0.54	0.69	1.04	2.23	2.79
Potassium	g%	0.65	3.90	5.70	4.20	3.30	10.60	4.50	3.30	9.50
Magnesium	g%	3.05	1.98	1.82	3.05	1.96	1.67	1.65	2.04	1.27
Calcium	mg%	576.00	869.00	906.00	1162.00	1035.00	954.00	1096.00	350.00	310.00
Phosphorus	mg%	53.00	457.00	488.00	195.00	283.00	358.00	171.00	510.00	240.00
Iron	mg%	278.00	11.00	8.00	43.00	4.00	7.00	12.00	74.00	40.00
Manganese	mg%	14.00	NT	NT	T	NT	NT	NT	4.00	113.00
Molybdenum	ppm	3.80	1.70	NT	NT	1.90	2.20	NT	NT	1.60
Selenium	ppm	0.076	0.085	0.128	0.159	0.031	0.035	0.031	0.134	0.070

Note: T = trace;   NT = no trace.

Sea Vegetable	Common Name
Monostroma latissimum	awo-nori
Analipus japonicus	hijiki
Undaria pinnatifida	wakame
Laminaria angustata	mitsuishi-kombu
Laminaria japonica	ma-kombu
Porphyra yezoensis	nori
Gracilaria verrucosa	ogo

Analysis extracted from Johnston, H. W. " A Detailed Chemical Analysis of Some Edible Japanese Seaweeds," in Proceedings of the Seventh International Seaweed Symposium; Sophora, Japan; August 1971; Kazutou, Nisazawa, Editor in Chief. pp. 429-435. Permission from John Wiley and Sons, 1974, Trondheim, New York.

Part II

From Shore to Stove

Table 6

Explanations of Ingredients Used And Some Suggested Substitutions

Sea Vegetable	How Used	Dried Substitute
Alaria	fresh, dry, frozen	Alaria, or wakame
Laminaria	fresh, dry, frozen	kelp, kombu-many types
Gracilaria	fresh, frozen	possibly dulse
Nereocystis	fresh, pickled	none
Pelvetiopsis	fresh, frozen	possibly hijiki
Porphyra	fresh, dry, frozen	nori
Cystoseira	fresh, dry	possibly hijiki

Other Ingredients Available In Health Food Stores or Food Co-ops

Tofu: Soybean curd. A four ounce serving of tofu made with nigari or calcium sulfate coagulant provides 74 calories, 9 grams of protein, 4.7 grams of fat, 2.3 grams of carbohydrate, 145 milligrams of calcium and 4.1 milligrams of iron.

Tempeh: A firm block of fermented soybean bound by mold culture. Four ounce tempeh has 170 calories, 17 grams of protein, 6 grams of fat, 13 grams of carbohydrate, plus vitamin B_{12}, B_2, B_5, folic acid, iron and phosphorus. Tempeh can be made at home with purchased culture. Look for it in the frozen food section of health (natural) food stores.

Miso: "Fermented soybean paste," a savory high protein seasoning in three basic types.

Tamari: (more properly called shoyu) Japanese fermented soy sauce is made from soybeans, cracked roasted wheat, aspergillus mold, salt and water. It is much superior to the domestic synthetic soy sauce.

Spike: A mixture of many herbs, seasonings and salt. Available in health food stores.

CHAPTER FIVE

SEA VEGETABLE DESCRIPTIONS & RECIPES

Ideas for the recipes in this book have not only come from various sources, but from wild inspiration. While experimenting with a new dish or even a variation of one, I often felt like a child squealing and delighting in her mudpies. But then credit must go to my long-suffering husband who ate almost everything put before him and seemed genuinely pleased most of the time, and whose reaction served a great role in finalizing the recipes that follow.

For those cooks who wish to go beyond experimenting with the recipes in this book, perhaps creating your own, or variations of those that follow, there are numerous considerations. For instance, in developing the recipe for Tofu *Alaria* Roll-ups, first was the discovery that seaweeds, used like an eggroll wrapper, cabbage or grape leaf, make a neat wrap for combinations of fillings. Second, the discovery that tofu is dramatically changed by freezing. Third, selecting filling ingredients, seasonings and liquids. Fourth, a method of cooking was selected (stove-top, oven, or pressure cooker), and last, the form of seaweed was choosen, fresh, dried, or commercial.

Whether you choose to follow the recipes exactly or bend them to your own individual tastes, please feel free to share your reactions and ideas with me. I would love to hear about your triumphs in creating new recipes, and even those disasters that eventually lead to victory.

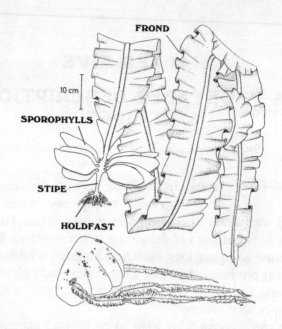

FROND

10 cm

SPOROPHYLLS

STIPE

HOLDFAST

Alaria marginata
(ah-Lair-ee-yah)

Alaria or winged kelp is sometimes found packaged dry, labeled "wakame," although true wakame is a different species, from Japan.

Description

Color: Olive brown to green

Size: 6 – 10 feet long (2 – 3m), 4 – 12 inches (10 – 30m) wide

Features: Large frond or blade with distinctive flattened midrib. At the base are paired sporophylls, which are small, thick, oval-shaped blades which produced the reproductive spores.

Alaria marginata

Habitat & Distribution

Coastal Area: *Alaria marginata* – Alaska to central California, *Alaria esculenta* – (East Coast) Arctic to Cape Cod

Tidal Condition: *Alaria marginata* – lower tidal zone on moderate to very rocky shores, *Alaria esculenta* – subtidal zone, occasionally in low intertidal zone on exposed rocks.

Foraging

Season: Late spring to autumn

Special Instructions: Blade should be cut above the reproductive sporophylls, leaving three feet of the blade to assure continued harvest and propagation.

Preparation

Preservation: Sun dry, store in tight plastic bags, or freeze (if frozen, use within three months). Dried *Alaria,* when reconstituted in water, is very much like the fresh plant. The fresh plant has a very short shelf life, even if refrigerated, so preserve soon after harvesting.

Uses

There are several interesting and delicious ways to prepare *Alaira,* as you will discover in the recipes. The chopped fresh midrib of this sea plant is a crunchy addition to salads. The sporophylls, when fried, are said to be reminiscent of peanuts. *Alaria,* with its mild flavor, may be used like spinach or cabbage, to roll around stuffings. It is one of the algae from which kelp meal for human nutrition is produced.

Nutrients

High in vitamin C, vitamin B_{12}, folic acid, niacin, pantothenic acid, calcium, vitamin B_5, plus protein, algin, nitrogen, magnesium, phosphorous, and essential trace elements. According to Madlener, it also may contain boron, radium, rubidium, cadmium, cobalt, and nickel. (See Table 5, p. 62, for the Japanese species, *Alaria crassifolia*) No recent analysis of American *Alaria* species using modern techniques are available.

Recipes follow. See also recipes for *Laminaria;* Krunchy Kelp and Kelp Powder or Flakes. *Alaria* flakes may also be used in *Porphyra* bread recipes.

Rice Bake with Meat

Quicker than Roll-ups to fix. A quick, nourishing rice meal inside a blanket of Alaria. Serves two.

1 large frond *Alaria*. Use fresh, frozen or dried. If frozen, thaw by placing in hot water. If dried, reconstitute by soaking in ½ cup water 15 minutes
¾ cup beef or pork sausage
¾ cup cooked rice
¼ cup chopped onion
¼ cup catsup or ½ cup seasoned tomato sauce

Cut *Alaria* frond into two sections to fit baking pan. Place one section in bottom of pan. Add sausage, broken into pieces, rice and onion. Fit remaining *Alaria* over top and dot with catsup or tomato sauce. Season if desired with Spike or Italian seasonings, especially if using unseasoned meat. Bake covered, 25 minutes at 350 degrees.

Rice Bake Vegetarian Style

Follow above recipe, except substitute a cup of tempeh cubes for the meat. Dip cubes in seasoning mixture below and fry until golden brown.

Seasoning mixture:
¼ cup water
1 teaspoon coriander
1 teaspoon grated garlic
1 teaspoon salt

Spanakopita

Inspired by a Greek dish, this recipe is not difficult to prepare. Pizza enthusiasts will love this nutritious and hearty meal!

2 cups fresh *Alaria*, sliced or chopped
1 teaspoon salt
3 cups cottage or ricotta cheese
3 eggs, beaten
1½ cups whole wheat flour and 1 cup white flour
¼ cup oil
1 cup warm water
1 teaspoon salt
½ cup margarine or butter, melted
1 pizza pan or two 9 inch pie tins

Wash and pat *Alaria* dry. Chop it rather fine. Sprinkle fresh *Alaria* with salt to wilt it.

Beat eggs, mix in cottage cheese and *Alaria*.

Mix flours, salt, oil and water, and knead briefly to make soft dough, adding more flour if necessary. Divide dough into two balls, one larger than the other. Roll out the larger one into a circle on a plastic cloth, about 3 inches larger than the pizza pan. If using pie tins, roll out 2 circles so that an inch or two hangs over the edge. Fold back edge so that it won't stretch and break while rolling out the top crust. Roll the small piece of dough for the top crust.

Unfold the edges of the lower crust and drizzle a few tablespoons of melted margarine over it. Put in the filling and drizzle a little of the margarine over it. Cover with the top crust, fold the under crust edge up around the top crust. Drizzle remaining margarine over top, especially the edges. Poke small holes in the top.

Bake on rack in the lower part of a 400 degree oven about 40 minutes, or until brown. Cover with towel and let stand a few minutes to set before serving. Cut in wedges. Serves 4 to 6.

Tempeh Vegetable Sauté

Use Alaria, Pelvetiopsis or Postelsia

1 cup packed dried *Alaria*, soaked in ½ cup water or 1½ cups
    fresh *Alaria*, *Pelvetiopsis* or *Postelsia*
1 medium onion thinly sliced
¾ cup sliced mushrooms
1 small green pepper, thinly sliced
1½ cup sliced carrots
1½ cup edible pod peas, if available
12 ounces tempeh, cut into 1 x 1½ x ¼ inch pieces, dipped
    into seasoning solution below and drained on paper towel
oil for frying
2 tablespoons shoyu
1 teaspoon spike
⅛ teaspoon pepper

Seasoning Solution:
½ cup water
2 cloves garlic, grated
1 teaspoon coriander
1 teaspoon salt

Thinly slice seaweed. Combine ingredients for seasoning solution. Dip tempeh slices, drain briefly on absorbent paper. Heat oil in wok, skillet or deep fryer to 325 degrees. Fry tempeh 3 to 4 minutes until crisp and golden brown. Drain on toweling. Strain oil and use 3 tablespoons for sautéing onion and *Alaria* about 4 minutes. Add mushrooms, carrots and green pepper and sauté 3 minutes longer. Add tempeh, shoyu and pepper and spike; mix well. Serve hot or cold.

Rice Mushroom Soup Casserole

1 cup dried *Alaria* – cut into pieces
2 cups brown rice
2 cups cold water and 2 cups hot water
1 can undiluted cream of mushroom soup or Mushroom
    Sauce below
1 tablespoon shoyu

Soak *Alaria* and rice in 2 cups cold water for two hours. Add 2 cups hot water and bring to boil. Lower heat and cook until partially tender. Put into casserole or baking pan. Mix in shoyu. Top with mushroom soup or sauce and bake, covered, about 45 minutes or until rice is done.

Mushroom Sauce:
1½ tablespoon melted butter
½ teaspoon salt
3 tablespoons finely chopped onions
¾ cups finely chopped mushrooms
1½ tablespoons flour, barley or whole wheat
1½ cups chicken broth or bouillon

Sauté mushrooms and onions in butter. Add flour, stirring. Add stock and continue cooking until thickened.

Alaria Soyfood Delight

1 cup brown rice
2 cups water
6 tablespoons tamari (shoyu) soy sauce
4 to 5 tablespoons oil
1 pound tofu, or 8 ounces tempeh cut into small pieces

1 medium onion, chopped

2 cups *Alaria* (about 1 ounce dried) loosely packed into cup

2 cups vegetables (use celery sliced thin, bean sprouts, zucchini, snow peas, green pepper or broccoli, etc. or a combination)

¾ cup jack cheese, sliced

Cook rice in 2 cups water with 1 tablespoon tamari. If using tempeh, sauté tempeh in 2 tablespoons oil until light brown and crisp. Remove and place on bottom of casserole. Add 3 tablespoons tamari. If using tofu, marinate pieces in casserole with 3 tablespoons tamari.

Soak dried *Alaria* in water. Drain and slice thinly. Sauté onion. Add *Alaria*, sauté briefly. Add 2 tablespoons tamari and cook gently a few minutes until tender. Remove and layer on top of soyfood in casserole. Sauté remaining vegetables briefly and layer on top of *Alaria*. Place rice on top of vegetables, and top with layer of cheese. Bake 20 minutes at 350 degrees.

Chicken Favorite

1 large frying chicken

2 cups dried sea vegetable cut into ½ inch pieces, or use 4 cups fresh

½ onion, chopped

2 cups rice (brown is best)

¼ cup shoyu (soy sauce)

2 cloves garlic, minced

1 teaspoon Hot Seas Seasoning (see recipe)

about 2 quarts water

Soak cut dry seaweed in water until it swells. Add chicken and garlic and simmer until chicken is tender. Remove chicken and debone, set aside. Add rice, shoyu, onions and seasoning to broth, and cook until rice is done. Add chicken meat, and let flavors mingle about 15 minutes.

Lasagne or Pizza

Meat or vegetarian; serves 8 to 10.

2 to 3 large pizza crusts, or 12 ounce lasagne noodles and 2 to 3 quarts boiling water, with 1 teaspoon salt added
10 to 12 ounces tempeh, thawed and cut into ¼ inch pieces, or 1 pound hamburger
2 tablespoons oil
1 onion, diced
1 green pepper, diced
1 cup sliced mushrooms
2 cloves garlic, minced
2 cups cottage cheese or 1 pound tofu, mash or blend
4 teaspoons mixed Italian spices (oregano, basil, marjoram, etc.)
4 cups canned or stewed tomatoes
8 ounce can tomato sauce
2 cups chopped fresh *Alaria* or 1 ounce dried *Alaria*, reconstituted in juice from tomatoes and chopped
¼ teaspoon cayenne
½ to 1 pound jack cheese, sliced
salt to taste
3 to 4 tomatoes, sliced, for pizza variation

Sauté tempeh or hamburger in oil. Add onion, green pepper, mushrooms, and simmer 5 minutes. Add herbs and other seasonings, tomatoes and tomato sauce, chopped *Alaria*, and simmer 15 minutes, or 1 to 1½ hours until thick for pizza variation.

Lasagne: Arrange two alternate layers of noodles and tomato mixture and cheese, topping with noodles and cheese. Bake at 350 degrees 30 to 45 minutes. Let stand 5 minutes before serving.

Pizza: Prepare 2 or 3 pizza crusts, following recipe for sourdough pizza. Divide tomato mixture onto pizza crusts. Bake in 400 to 450 degree oven about 10 minutes, until almost done. Top with sliced tomatoes and cheese, and continue baking until cheese is melted.

Tortillas with Alaria Lentil Spread

3 tablespoons oil
⅓ cup grated garlic
1 cup dried lentils, soaked in 1 cup water, 1½ to 2 hours
3 large tomatoes, chopped
1 cup water
2 tablespoons tamari (soy sauce)
3 tablespoons grape juice, or sake or sherry and 1 teaspoon honey
1 teaspoon cumin
1 teaspoon Spike, or mixture of thyme and oregano
1 cup dried *Alaria*, softened in water and chopped or cut into small pieces
chili powder to taste, about ½ teaspoon

In heavy enamel pot or skillet, heat oil and lightly sauté garlic. Add lentils, *Alaria*, tomatoes, sautéing each in turn. Add remaining seasonings and water. Cover and simmer until lentils are tender, about 30 minutes. Serve with tortillas.

Note: A delicious tortilla-like bread may be made with raised sourdough. (See recipe for *Porphyra* sourdough bread for pizza or French bread.) Use about the same amount as for a bun, and roll very thin on board sprinkled with fine corn meal.

Let rise a few minutes, and bake in hot oven on greased pans, removing while still soft enough to roll around the filling when making enchiladas.

Enchiladas

About 6 tortillas with lentil spread recipe, above.
1 cup sliced or grated jack cheese

Follow above recipe, rolling lentil filling in tortillas. Top with sliced jack cheese. Bake in shallow pan or dish about 20 minutes at 350 degrees.

Stuffed Zucchini

1 large but tender zucchini, about 1 to 1½ foot in length or use
    several smaller zucchinis
1½ ounce dried *Alaria* (about 2 large fronds)
1 quart fresh or canned mashed tomatoes, or tomato sauce
1 onion, diced
1½ cup cooked garbanzo beans, corn, or cooked rice
2 cloves garlic, grated
1 pound ground meat, or tempeh cut into ¼ inch pieces
1 to 2 tablespoons mixed Italian seasoning (marjoram, basil,
    oregano)
¼ teaspoon cayenne
salt to taste
½ cup chopped mushrooms (opt.)
¼ cup green bell pepper, diced (opt.)
2 tablespoons oil
1 cup grated cheese (opt.)

Soak *Alaria* in tomatoes about 30 minutes. Remove and chop. Brown meat or tempeh in oil. Add onions, mushrooms, and sauté lightly. Add remaining ingredients and simmer a few minutes.

Remove pulp and seeds from zucchini by cutting off a length-wise strip and scooping out the middle, leaving the ends and skin in place. Arrange zucchini in covered roasting pan or casserole. Fill with stuffing. Add boiling liquid or tomato juice, ½ inch deep in pan around the zucchini. Bake at 350 degrees, 1 hour or more, until zucchini is tender. May be sprinkled with grated cheese (jack, cheddar, or parmesan).

Note: It may be desirable to scoop out some of the zucchini meat, especially if rather mature, but leave enough to hold the zucchini shape. Cut meat up, and cook along with other ingredients before stuffing shell.

Creamed Alaria With Yogurt

1 cup fresh or frozen *Alaria*, or ½ ounce dried *Alaria* or
　　wakame reconstituted in ¼ cup water
¼ cup water for cooking *Alaria*
½ cup yogurt
1 clove garlic, minced
1 teaspoon tamari (soy sauce)
1 teaspoon lemon juice
½ teaspoon dill
1 teaspoon margarine (opt.)
2 tablespoons toasted sesame seeds (opt.)

Chop *Alaria* fine, put in saucepan with water. Simmer about 10 minutes, until tender. Drain. Blend yogurt, soy sauce, lemon juice, dill and garlic. Pour onto *Alaria*. Add margarine. Serve alone, or atop rice or French pancakes. Sprinkle with toasted sesame seeds.

Creamed Alaria With Tofu

Follow above recipe, substituting ¼ pound tofu for yogurt, and add ½ cup diced fresh tomato. Blend tofu with seasonings in blender and pour over cooked *Alaria*. Heat and serve alone or over rice or French pancakes, sprinkled with toasted sesame seeds.

Creamed Alaria With White Sauce

1 cup fresh or frozen *Alaria* or ½ ounce dried *Alaria* or wakame
½ cup water
1 hard cooked egg
3 tablespoons butter
1 tablespoon finely chopped onion
2½ tablespoons flour
1 cup cream or evaporated milk
seasoning to taste – salt, paprika, mustard, grated lemon rind
    or ½ teaspoon nutmeg, according to preference
½ cup grated Swiss, or 2 tablespoons parmesan cheese, or
    ¼ package (2 ounces) crumbled cream cheese (opt.)

Reconstitute dried *Alaria* 15 minutes in water. Cook *Alaria* about 10 minutes or until tender. Chop or puree in blender. Melt margarine in skillet. Add onion and flour and blend. Slowly stir in hot cream or milk. When sauce is smooth and boiling add the *Alaria*. Stir and cook 3 minutes or so. Add cheese if desired. Season and serve garnished with slices of hard cooked eggs. (See recipe for French pancakes filled with creamed *Alaria*.)

Alaria Souffle

½ to 1 ounce dried *Alaria*, or 1 – 2 cups fresh *Alaria*
1 tablespoon tamari (soy sauce)
1 pint cottage cheese
4 eggs, separated
4 tablespoons flour
1 cup grated cheese (feta, cheddar or jack)
juice of 1 lemon
dash pepper or cayenne
2 tablespoons Italian herbs, such as thyme, oregano, marjoram,
    or 2 teaspoons Spike seasoning
1 clove garlic
1 tablespoon minced onion (opt.)

Soak dried *Alaria* a short time in ½ to ¾ cups water. (Use larger amount of water for larger seaweed amount.) Add tamari, and bring to boil. Simmer gently about 10 minutes until tender. Chop *Alaria* in blender with cottage cheese until smooth. Blend in egg yolk, flour, garlic, lemon juice and seasonings. Beat egg whites until stiff and fold in the blended *Alaria* mixture. Put into casserole or ring mold and bake at 350 degrees about 45 minutes until set.

(H) Alarious Carrots

½ cup dried *Alaria* snipped into small pieces (use fresh *Alaria*
    when available)
½ cup water
1 cup sliced carrots
½ teaspoon dill
salt to taste
¼ teaspoon ground cloves (opt.)

Soak dried *Alaria* 10 minutes in water. (If using fresh, slice into strips.) Add dill, bring to boil, and turn down heat. Simmer 10 minutes. Add carrots and continue cooking 10 minutes.

(H)Alarious Potatoes

½ cup dried *Alaria* (fresh *Alaria* may be used if available)
1 cup water
4 medium potatoes, peeled and cut into chunks

Snip *Alaria* into small pieces with scissors, or if using fresh *Alaria* slice across into thin strips. Soak dried *Alaria* in water a few minutes to soften and reconstitute. Combine *Alaria* with potatoes and water. Bring to boil. Reduce heat and cook until potatoes are tender. Season with butter and salt.

Succotash

1 cup fresh *Alaria*, chopped, or ½ cup dry *Alaria* cut into little
    pieces and softened in small amount of water
½ cup dry lima beans (makes about 1 cup cooked beans)
1 cup whole kernel corn
2 tablespoons chopped onion
¼ green or red bell pepper, sliced
½ teaspoon chili powder
½ teaspoon Spike or oregano
1 tablespoon parsley, chopped or 1 teaspoon dry parsley flakes

To cook lima beans, rinse, then bring to boil in 1½ cups water. Remove from heat and let stand an hour, then boil gently until tender. Sauté onion and pepper. Add lima beans, corn, *Alaria*, and seasonings and simmer 5 minutes. Serve hot.

Tempeh Triumph

1 ounce (approx.) dried *Alaria*, or 1 to 2 fresh fronds
4 tablespoons oil
1 pound tempeh
1 onion, diced
1 green pepper, diced
2 to 3 cloves garlic, minced
29 ounce can tomato puree
2 to 3 tablespoons each of vinegar, molasses and tamari
½ teaspoon powdered mustard
1 teaspoon grated ginger root

Soak *Alaria* frond 30 minutes in water. Drain and cut into strips 2½ inches wide. Cut tempeh into 2½ inch strips. Sauté in 2 to 3 tablespoons oil until browned. Remove.

Sauté green pepper, onion, and garlic. Add remaining ingredients except *Alaria* and simmer 15 minutes. Add tempeh strips and continue simmering 20 minutes.

Wrap tempeh in *Alaria* strips. Place in large baking dish, top with remaining sauce, cover with foil and bake 25 minutes at 350 degrees. (May also be made simply by layering *Alaria*, tempeh and sauce.)

Tempeh Turkey

A barb'qued vegetarian turkey for Thanksgiving!

1 very large zucchini: one of the "wild" escapers that every
   gardener discovers hiding under the vine – it should be
   still tender and measure about 14 to 18 inches in length
1½ ounce dried *Alaria* or 3 to 4 fronds fresh *Alaria*
1 cup *Nereocystis*, preserved without sugar (see pickle recipe)
   or use fresh *Nereocystis*
2 pounds tempeh, cut into pieces about 1½ x 1 x ½ inch
2 cups sliced mushrooms
1 ½ onion, chopped (about 1½ cups)
4 cloves garlic, grated
½ green pepper, chopped
1 quart tomatoes, canned
40 ounces tomato sauce
¼ teaspoon cayenne
2 tablespoons Spike
2 tablespoons Italian seasonings
1¼ cup each vinegar, shoyu and molasses
oil for sautéing

Cut "Turkey" zucchini in half lengthwise, making one
half slightly bigger, for the body of the bird. The top half will
be used to fashion a head and fan-shaped tail as illustrated.
Scoop out the seeds and pulp from the body of the turkey. Pare
out some of the meat, but leave plenty of support. Turn upside
down on baking sheet and bake till slightly soft. (Don't
overbake or it will collapse when filled.) Heat oil in large
skillet or wok. Sauté tempeh pieces until lightly brown.
Remove tempeh and sauté onions, garlic; add green pepper
and zucchini meat. Continue cooking.

Soak dried *Alaria* about 15 minutes in tomatoes to soften.
Chop *Alaria*, and add all remaining ingredients to skillet,
including tempeh, and continue simmering until flavors are
blended, and the volume concentrated.

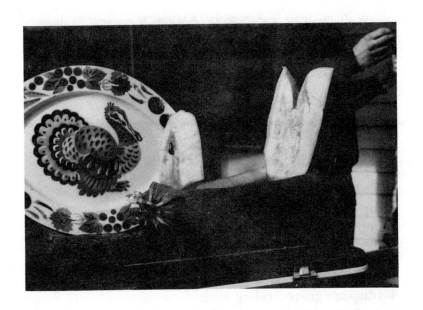

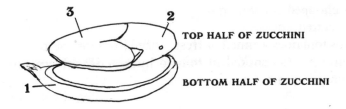

TOP HALF OF ZUCCHINI

BOTTOM HALF OF ZUCCHINI

Tempeh Turkey.

Stuff "turkey body." Bake about 1 hour at 350 degrees until body of turkey is tender, but not soft. Place the baked head and tail piece at ends of the body of the turkey, inside the shell. Decorate head with a cranberry for the eye.

Garbanzo Roll-ups

1½ ounce *Alaria* (about 2 large fronds, dried or fresh)
1 cup tomato juice
¾ cup brown rice, cooked in 1¾ cups water until tender
1 cup dry garbanzo beans, cooked (makes 1½ cups)
½ to ⅔ cup yogurt
2 tablespoons chopped fresh chives
¼ teaspoon ground celery seeds
1 teaspoon mixed Italian herbs or Spike
1 tablespoon tamari (soy sauce)
¼ cup chopped celery
1 cup chopped mushrooms
⅔ cup grated cheese
1½ cups tomatoes, canned or fresh, sliced (for more protein, ⅓
    cup soy grits soaked in tomato juice and 2 tablespoons
    brewer's yeast may be added)

Soak dried *Alaria* fronds in tomato juice about 30 minutes. Cut into 5 to 6 inch segments. Blend garbanzos and yogurt in blender until the mixture is smooth.

In mixing bowl combine garbanzo mixture with rice, parsley, chives, herbs, celery, mushrooms, soy grits and brewer's yeast, if used. Place 2 to 3 tablespoons of the stuffing in each *Alaria* segment. Fold up to cover the stuffing.

Place in baking dish, top with tomatoes and cheese, add remaining tomato juice and bake covered in 350 degree oven about 30 minutes, adding more tomato liquid or water if necessary.

Frozen Tofu Roll-ups

1 pound frozen tofu cut into pieces about 2½ x 1 x ½ inches
6 pieces of *Alaria* cut 2½ x 6 inches, or substitute kombu or
  wakame
1 cup stock (use water from soaking dried *Alaria*)
1½ tablespoons shoyu
2 tablespoons honey
1 tablespoon mirin, sake, sherry or grape juice

In the process of freezing, tofu is transformed into a spongy, highly absorbent and cohesive product, which readily absorbs other flavors when simmered or sautéed. Freezing not only changes tofu into a completely new food with unique uses in cooking, but makes it possible to preserve this highly perishable food. It may be stored up to six months wrapped in plastic. Thaw by placing frozen tofu in bowl with several quarts of hot water, for 5 to 10 minutes. Pour off hot water and add cold water. Press with hands to expel hot water. Lift out of water and press firmly to remove water.

For this recipe it is easier to cut the pieces of tofu before freezing. They need not be thawed before wrapping and cooking.

Reconstitute *Alaria* by dipping in water a few minutes. Save liquid for stock. Cut into pieces and roll each piece of tofu in a piece of sea vegetable. Place roll-ups in pressure cooker with remaining ingredients. Cook 15 minutes at 15 pounds pressure. Remove from heat and allow to cool naturally. Roll-ups may be served hot or chilled in the broth before serving.

Tofu Italian Seaweed Rolls

2 to 3 fronds *Alaria* or *Pleurophycus*
12 ounces tofu, drained
¼ cup chopped walnut meats
1 medium onion, minced
⅓ cup bread crumbs
1 egg
1 tablespoon dried parsley flakes
1½ tablespoon red miso or ½ teaspoon salt
oil for deep frying
2 cups canned or stewed tomatoes or tomato sauce
⅓ cup tomato catsup
1 teaspoon oregano
½ cup jack cheese or ¼ cup grated parmesan cheese

If using fresh seaweed, steam briefly and cut into 4 to 5 inch pieces. If using dried seaweed, soak in water, tomato juice or sauce 20 minutes, and cut into 4 to 5 inch pieces. Combine tofu, nut meats, onion, bread crumbs, egg and parsley and 1 teaspoon red miso or salt. Mix thoroughly and shape into 10 to 12 balls.

In small pan, wok, skillet, or deep fryer, heat oil to about 350 degrees, hot enough to brown the balls when they are added to it. Deep fat fry until well browned. Drain on towel. Place each ball onto a seaweed square. Roll up and place in casserole or baking pan. Combine tomatoes or tomato sauce, catsup, ½ tablespoon miso and oregano and pour on top of seaweed balls. Top with cheese and bake covered, at 350 degrees about 45 minutes.

Alaria with Rice Casserole

½ to 1 can undiluted cream of mushroom soup
1 cup *Alaria* (dried) cut into pieces
2 cups brown rice
4 cups water

Soak *Alaria* and rice in 2 cups water 2 hours. Add 2 cups hot water and cook until partially tender. Mix in soup. Put into casserole or baking pan, and bake 30 minutes at 350 degrees.

Rice Meat Roll-ups

Burgers in Blankets

3 large fronds of *Alaria*. If using dried *Alaria*, reconstitute in water about 15 minutes. If using fresh *Alaria*, steam 1 minute to soften. Save water for soup.

1 pound hamburger	2 cups cooked rice
½ onion, chopped	1 egg, beaten
2 cloves garlic, minced	1 cup mushrooms, chopped
1 teaspoon shoyu (tamari)	either 2 cups tomato juice or
1 teaspoon Spike	2 cups water plus
	2 tablespoons shoyu

Blanch *Alaria* or reconstitute dried *Alaria* – cut into 6 inch lengths. Fry hamburger gently. Remove fat, and continue frying with onion, garlic and seasonings. Combine meat mixture with rice and egg. Form into 2 inch balls and roll a piece of *Alaria* around each ball. Place in shallow pan, cover with 2 cups tomato juice or water and shoyu. Sprinkle with more Spike (1 teaspoon). Cover with lid or foil and bake 45 minutes at 325 degrees.

Rice Roll-ups – Greek Style

Vegetarian

3 large fronds of *Alaria*. If using dried *Alaria*, reconstitute in water about 15 minutes. If using fresh *Alaria*, steam 1 minute to soften (save water for soup).

½ onion, chopped	2 cups cooked rice
1 teaspoon shoyu (tamari)	1 egg, beaten
1½ cups cottage cheese	1 cup mushrooms, chopped
¼ cup oil	2 cups water plus 2 tablespoons
¾ cup raisins	shoyu and 1 teaspoon Spike
1 teaspoon dill	

Blanch *Alaria* or reconstitute dried *Alaria*, and cut into 6 inch lengths. Sauté onions and mushrooms in oil. Combine with cottage cheese, raisins, dill, rice and egg. Form into 2 inch balls and roll a piece of *Alaria* around each ball. Place in shallow pan, cover with 2 cups water and shoyu. Cover with lid or foil and bake 45 minutes at 325 degrees.

Middle East Style Roll-ups

2 fronds *Alaria* (dried, fresh or frozen)
2 tablespoons parsley flakes
½ cup uncooked brown rice
1 large tomato, peeled
¼ cup green onion or shallot tops, chopped
1 small onion, chopped
¼ cup chopped *Nereocystis* Dill Pickles
¼ cup liquid from *Nereocystis* Dill Pickles

pepper and other spices, such as cinnamon, allspice, or mint, if
desired

¼ cup salad oil (use olive oil for true Mid-East flavor)

½ cup *Alaria* stock and ½ cup liquid from *Nereocystis* Dill
Pickles

Reconstitute dried *Alaria* by soaking in cup of water for a
few minutes. Cut into pieces approximately 4 x 6 inches. Mix
chopped vegetables with rice, salad oil, dill pickles, pickle juice
and oil. Place 1 tablespoon filling on each *Alaria* piece,
spreading to ½ inch of edge. Roll, folding in both ends after
first roll to secure filling. Make them fairly uniform in size,
about ¾ inch in diameter.

Arrange in compact rows on a rack in pressure cooker
with *Alaria* or other stock and *Nereocystis* Dill Pickle liquid.
Cook 25 minutes at 15 pounds pressure. Cool naturally. These
also could be cooked on top the stove with more liquid and a
tight cover, or baked, covered in an oven at 350 degrees, about
1½ hours. Serve hot or cold.

Middle East Style Roll-ups With Meat

To above recipe add 1 cup ground uncooked meat, such as
hamburger or lamb, to the rice and vegetables. Omit oil.

The above recipes attempt to capture the delightful
appearance and flavors of a Lebanese dish we enjoyed at a
restaurant in Seattle. On consulting a Lebanese recipe book, I
found the recipes usually included chopped lamb, pine nuts
and lemon juice. Since the recipes presented here have none of
these, I suppose they're hardly authentic. The Lebanese
recipes for stuffed cabbage rolls call for cinnamon, allspice and
mint. I'd like to try these spices in this recipe some day – about
¼ teaspoon of each. The recipes were adapted from a Lebanese

recipe for Lenton Stuffed Grape Leaves. Chopped *Nereocystis* Dill Pickles and liquid replace lemon and salt, and *Alaria* serves for the grape leaves.

Bean Bags

Makes 14 to 16 rolls.

2 to 3 fronds *Alaria* (if dried, reconstitute by soaking in ½ cup
    water 15 minutes)
1½ cup cooked rice
½ cup cooked lentils or adzuki beans
½ cup cottage cheese or ricotta cheese
1 cup jack cheese cubes
4 ounce tomato paste (about ½ cup)
2 eggs, beaten
1 clove garlic, minced
1½ cups tempeh cubes
1 cup mushrooms, sliced
2 to 3 tablespoons oil
1 tablespoon shoyu (soy sauce)
2 teaspoons vinegar
1 teaspoon Spike
¼ teaspoon celery seed
2 cups canned or fresh sliced tomatoes

Steam fresh *Alaria* 1 to 2 minutes to soften or reconstitute dried *Alaria* in water. Cut into 4 to 5 inch strips. Cook approximately ½ cup brown rice and ½ cup lentils or beans in 2 cups water to make the rice and bean combination. Sauté mushrooms and tempeh in oil. Add shoyu and vinegar. Combine rice, bean, tempeh, cheese, beaten eggs, tomato paste and seasonings. Place about 2 to 3 teaspoons rice mixture on each strip of *Alaria* and roll with midrib around middle. Place in 9 x 10 baking pan or casserole. Top with tomatoes. Cover with lid or foil. Bake 30 minutes at 350 degrees.

Corn Roll-ups

3 to 4 fronds *Alaria*, fresh or dried (about 2 cups packed)
1 can whole kernel corn, drained
2 tablespoons dry milk powder
2 slices whole wheat bread made into crumbs
¼ cup minced onion
2 eggs, beaten or ½ pound beef or pork sausage
½ teaspoon celery seed
1 cup grated cheese
2 teaspoons Spike, or Italian type herbs (marjoram, thyme, oregano)
16 ounce tomato sauce plus ½ cup water
2 cloves garlic, minced

Mix corn, milk powder, bread crumbs, egg and celery seed. Steam fresh *Alaria* 1 to 2 minutes, or reconstitute dried *Alaria* in water about 15 minutes. Cut into 6 inch pieces. In each piece of *Alaria* wrap 2 tablespoons corn mixture formed into balls.

Place in casserole or baking pan and cover with tomato sauce mixed with water, garlic and herbs. Sprinkle cheese on top (or cheese may be added to corn mixture). Bake in covered casserole at 325 degrees or cook in covered skillet on top of stove, about 45 minutes.

Note: Rice may be substituted for corn. Use 1 cup rice cooked in 2 cups water.

Curried Tempeh Indonesian

1½ cups *Alaria* (use fresh, frozen, or dried, 2 to 3 fronds)
2 cloves garlic
2 cups unsweetened coconut flakes or grated unsweetened
  coconut
2½ cups hot water
small piece ginger
1 teaspoon salt
½ teaspoon cloves
½ teaspoon coriander
¼ teaspoon cayenne
½ teaspoon turmeric
1 teaspoon brown sugar
1½ cups tempeh cubes
2 cups cooked rice

Slice fresh or rehydrated dried *Alaria.* Cook gently in small amount water about 5 minutes until tender. Set aside.

Prepare coconut milk by combining coconut, garlic, coriander with about half the hot water. Blend at high speed in blender a few miutes. Strain and repeat with remaining water, letting the coconut stand in the water, and heating gently a few minutes each time. Strain and discard pulp. Combine milk with tempeh, seasonings and *Alaria* and simmer 12 to 15 minutes. Serve over rice.

Cream of Alaria Soup

4 to 5 potatoes
1½ cup sliced or chopped zucchini
¾ cup *Alaria,* packed in cup
2 cups water
1 large clove garlic (plus small tender garlic plants or leeks if
  available)

1 onion chopped
2 teaspoons Spike (or basil plus Italian seasonings)
½ teaspoon celery seed
½ cup chicken stock or chicken flavoring
3 cups milk
½ cup non-fat dry milk powder
½ cup grated cheese

Soften *Alaria* in water. Bring to boil *Alaria*, zucchini, garlic, onion, spices and chicken flavoring. Cook slowly until vegetables are tender. Blend in blender with milk and milk powder. Add cheese and heat. Recipe may be varied with other sea and land vegetables.

Miso Soup with Tofu and Alaria

2 small onions, chopped
2 carrots, sliced
2 stalks celery – about 1 cup, sliced
1 quart water plus vegetarian bouillon, or use stock
¾ pound firm tofu, cubed
1 cup *Alaria*, soaked in water to soften, sliced; or 2 cups chopped spinach or other greens
2 cups any vegetable combination (chopped pepper, green beans, cabbage, mushrooms, zucchini, etc.)
2 tablespoons tahini
½ cup red miso
Spike, salt, and pepper to taste

Put vegetables into pot with water or stock, and bring to simmer. Cook until vegetables are tender (about 8 to 10 minutes). Add tofu cubes. Remove ½ cup soup broth and combine with miso and tahini to make paste. Stir paste into soup.

Split Pea Soup

1 cup dried split peas
5 to 6 cups water
½ cup dried *Alaria* (or substitute wakame)
1 to 2 carrots, sliced in chunks
1 medium onion, sliced
2 tablespoons sesame seed paste (tahini; opt.)
½ cup ham pieces (opt.)
salt to taste
mineral seasoning, such as Spike
2 cloves garlic

Simmer split peas in water until partially tender (about 1 hour). Soak *Alaria* in 1 cup water about 15 minutes. Add to peas with carrots, onion, garlic, spices, and ham if used. Simmer to creamy consistency, about 40 minutes. Remove from heat. Stir in sesame paste, if used. Salt to taste.

Tempeh Soup Indonesian

2 tablespoons oil
½ medium onion, chopped
1 clove garlic, grated
1 large green chillie thinly sliced, or ½ teaspoon cayenne
1 cup tempeh cut into ½ inch cubes
2 tablespoons sunflower seeds (opt.)
¾ cup thinly sliced green beans
1 cup *Alaria* pieces soaked 15 minutes in ½ cup water or 1½
    cup fresh *Alaria*, sliced
½ teaspoon ground coriander
1¾ cups (approx.) coconut milk as prepared below
2 cups soup stock or chicken flavored stock or water
2 tablespoons Vietnam style fish stock, or 1 teaspoon shrimp
    or fish paste

1 to 2 cups cooked rice
½ teaspoon fresh ginger, grated

Prepare coconut milk either from grated fresh coconut or flaked unsweetened dry coconut as follows: Use ½ cup fresh or ¾ cup dried coconut. Add about 1 cup very hot water and let stand 5 minutes. Puree in blender a minute or so. Strain through fine seive into bowl. Repeat process with 1 cup more hot water. Discard pulp.

Heat oil in wok or large skillet. Sauté onions, garlic, ginger, green beans, chillies, tempeh and sunflower seeds until tempeh is brown. Add *Alaria* and coriander and sauté 3 minutes longer. Remove from heat. Bring the stock to a boil. Add contents from wok and continue cooking gently 2 minutes. Stir in coconut milk and fish stock and simmer 3 minutes longer. Serve over rice.

Lentil-Tempeh Soup with Alaria

A hearty, full-flavored, high protein soup.

1 cup dried *Alaria*, cut into pieces (use scissors)
6 cups water or stock
1 cup lentils
6 ounces tempeh, cut into cubes
1 cup carrot pieces
2 or 3 cloves elephant garlic, cut into small pieces
2 teaspoons Spike
1 or 2 teaspoons cumin, coriander and chili powder
½ teaspoon each oregano, basil and marjoram
1 tablespoon soy sauce (opt.)
2 eight ounce cans tomato sauce, or 4 or 5 tomatoes, peeled
    and quartered (opt.)

Allow *Alaria* to soften and expand in the water or stock before heating. Combine with remaining ingredients. Bring to boil and simmer 2 hours or until lentils are tender. Add salt if needed.

Hearty Tempeh Split Pea Soup

A very hearty high protein soup easy to fix for a crowd. Recipe below makes five large servings.

½ cup dried *Alaria* snipped into pieces (or use fresh seaweed)
5 cups water
1 cup split peas (8 ounces)
6 ounces tempeh
½ cup chopped onion
2 cloves elephant garlic, chopped
1 cup carrot chunks
1½ teaspoons each cumin, Spike and coriander
½ teaspoon oregano
¼ teaspoon celery seed
1 tablespoon soy sauce (shoyu)

Place *Alaria* with cold water in pot. Allow *Alaria* to reconstitute and soften 10 to 15 minutes. Add remaining ingredients and heat slowly. Simmer 1½ hours, or until split peas are tender. Add salt if needed.

Split Pea Minestrone

2 to 3 tablespoons oil
2 cloves garlic, chopped
1 onion, chopped
4 teaspoons Italian seasonings

1 teaspoon Spike
½ teaspoon paprika
¼ teaspoon cayenne, plus a few peppercorns
12 ounce can tomato sauce
1¼ cups fresh *Alaria* or 1 dried frond soaked in water (use
    water for soup)
1 to 2 cups cooked garbanzos or kidney beans
1 cup cooked elbow macaroni
1 tablespoon parsley
1¼ cups split peas
2 quarts water
1½ cups zucchini, sliced
1 cup (approx.) each of carrots, sliced potatoes, and swiss chard
    or cabbage, sliced
¼ cup parmesan cheese (opt.)

Sauté onion and garlic. Stir in tomato sauce, peas, spices,
Alaria and water. Simmer 1 to 2 hours. Add carrots, potatoes
and garbanzos or beans. Simmer 30 minutes. Add macaroni,
zucchini and chard or cabbage. Simmer 10 minutes and serve,
topped with parmesan cheese.

Zucchini-Potato Soup with Alaria

4 to 5 potatoes
1½ cups sliced or chopped zucchini
¾ cup *Alaria*, packed in cup
2 cups water
1 large clove garlic (plus small tender garlic plants or leeks if
    available)
1 onion chopped
2 teaspoons Spike
½ teaspoon celery seed
½ cup chicken stock or chicken flavoring

3 cups milk
½ cup non-fat dry milk powder
½ cup grated cheese

Soften *Alaria* in water. Bring to boil *Alaria,* potatoes, zucchini, garlic, onion, spices and chicken flavoring. Cook slowly until vegetables are tender. Blend in blender with milk and milk powder. Add cheese and heat.

Squash Soup

This delicious golden and green soup combines the hearty texture of winter squash with flakes of nutritious Alaria.

½ cup dried *Alaria*
3 cups cooked winter squash
2½ cups water or vegetable stock
½ onion, chopped
1 tablespoon oil
½ cup chopped parsley or 2 tablespoons dry parsley flakes
1 teaspoon Hot Seas seasoning (see recipe) or ¼ teaspoon cayenne
1 teaspoon basil
1 cup dried skim milk
1 tablespoon nutritional yeast (opt.)

To prepare the squash and *Alaria:* Cut squash, remove seeds. Place squash and *Alaria* in pressure cooker with 3 to 4 cups water. Allow *Alaria* to soak a few minutes. Bring to pressure and cook 10 to 15 minutes, depending on thickness and hardness of squash. Remove peeling from squash and puree in blender with *Alaria* and liquid from the cooked squash and *Alaria.* Pour in soup pot and heat over low flame.
Sauté the onion in the oil. Add parsley and seasonings.

Cook briefly. Add to squash and *Alaria* mixture. Place 2 cups of squash mixture in blender with milk powder and yeast. Blend until smooth. Pour back into pot and heat on medium heat. Don't boil, or heat too fast, or it will stick.

Note: Soup may be made with left-over squash. (If you have squash already seasoned with cinnamon, this adds an interesting touch.) The *Alaria* should be cooked separately before pureeing with squash. To do this, reconstitute pieces of *Alaria* in water and bring to boil. Simmer about 15 minutes, until soft enough to puree.

Mushroom Hors d'Oeuvre

1 cup dried *Alaria* or wakame
3 cups chicken broth
¼ cup tamari soy sauce
½ onion, minced
5 cloves garlic, grated
1 teaspoon Italian seasonings
¼ teaspoon cayenne
1 pound large mushrooms
½ cup bread crumbs
½ cup grated cheese

Pull or cut out mushroom stems, leaving hollow caps. Dice stems.

Allow *Alaria* or wakame to reconstitute by soaking in chicken broth. Add garlic and soy sauce and half the chopped mushroom stems. Bring to boil and simmer about 30 minutes, or until tender. Puree sea vegetable in blender, using part of broth, as needed.

Sauté onion, garlic, and half of the diced mushroom stems. Add pureed sea vegetable and bread crumbs. Dip mushroom caps in melted margarine or butter. Fill them with pureed *Alaria* mixture, and sprinkle with cheese. Bake 15 to 20 minutes at 350 degrees.

Mushroom Barley Soup

2 cups water
1 cup dried *Alaria* cut into ½ inch pieces
½ cup barley
1 potato, peeled
2 tablespoons oil
½ pound mushrooms
2 cloves garlic, grated
1 small onion (1 cup sliced)
½ cup diced celery
1 cup diced zucchini
1 carrot sliced
2½ cups water (additional to above)
2 tablespoons brown rice miso
3 tablespoons shoyu (soy sauce)
½ teaspoons each, tarragon and oregano
1 teaspoon parsley flakes
½ teaspoon Hot Seas Seasoning
½ pound tofu, cubed (opt.)
½ cup rich milk or cream

Soak *Alaria* a few minutes in water. Add barley and boil slowly until about half done (30 minutes). Add potato, cut up, and continue cooking until tender.

Sauté in oil mushrooms, garlic, onion, celery, zucchini and carrots. Add water and seasoning, and cook until vegetables are tender. Add rice-barley-seaweed mixture, part or all of which is mashed in processor or blender. Add remaining ingredients and simmer till flavors are blended. Adjust seasonings, adding more if desired.

Note: Fresh seaweed such as *Alaria*, bullwhip rings or dried nori which has been crisped, may be substituted for the dried *Alaria*.

Sugarless Cherry Pie

1 unbaked pie shell and top (below)
1½ cups pitted pie cherries
1 cup chopped *Alaria* (use fresh or dry fronds and/or
    sporophylls)
1 tablespoon tapioca
½ cup yogurt
½ cherry juice
3 to 5 tablespoons sugar or honey (or sweetener)
½ teaspoon almond flavoring
1 tablespoon butter

Mix together all ingredients. Let stand 15 minutes to soften the dried *Alaria* and tapioca. Fill pan lined with crust. Top with woven strips of crust. Bake about 40 minutes in 350 degree oven.

Crust:
2 cups flour
½ cup oil
¼ cup yogurt
½ teaspoon salt

Stir together ingredients and roll into 2 crusts between waxed paper. Fit one shell into 8 or 9 inch pie tin. Cut one crust into ½ inch strips and use to weave lattice top crust over filled shell.

Sugarless Rhubarb Pie

1 unbaked pie shell and top (recipe above)
1 cup dried *Alaria*, snipped into small pieces and packed into
    measure
1¼ cup diced rhubarb

1 cup cream or half and half
artificial sweetener equivalent to 1 cup sugar
1 tablespoon flour
2 eggs, beaten
¼ teaspoon nutmeg
2 tablespoons butter

Warm cream and soak *Alaria* 10 minutes. Add remaining ingredients. Place in pie shell and top with crust. Prick or cut design to let out steam or cut strips to make lattice top. Bake in 350 degree oven about 25 minutes.

Sugarless Apple Pie

1 unbaked pie shell and top
3 cups sliced apples
1 cup dried *Alaria* cut into ½ inch pieces
1 cup yogurt
1 tablespoon margarine
3 teaspoons cinnamon
½ teaspoon nutmeg
sweetener equivalent to 1 cup sugar

Combine ingredients and let stand 30 minutes to soften *Alaria*. Place in unbaked pie shell, top with crust, cut top to let out steam. Bake 45 minutes in 350 degree oven.

Mermaid O-PB Cookie Bars

¼ cup finely ground dried *Alaria* or wakame (first, crisp in oven), grind in food processor if available
½ cup ground raisins
½ cup sunflower seeds, toasted and chopped or ground

½ cup whole wheat flour
¾ cup firmly packed dark brown sugar
2 cups quick oats or ground rolled oats
½ cup dry milk powder
2½ teaspoons baking powder
1 large egg
½ cup peanut butter
1¼ cups water
1 teaspoon vanilla
⅓ cup oil (opt.)
1 to 2 cups chocolate, butterscotch, or carob chips (opt.)

Mix all ingredients except chips. Spread in 9 x 12 inch pan. Sprinkle chips on top. Bake for about 30 minutes. Cut into small squares.

Powerhouse Candy

¼ cup finely ground dried seaweed (*Alaria*, wakame, nori, or a mixture
½ cup ground raisins
½ cup sunflower seeds, toasted and finely chopped or ground
½ cup peanut butter
½ cup honey
2 cups ground rolled oats, or quick oats

Use food processor or blender to grind seaweed, raisins and sunflowers seeds. Mix ingredients well, form into balls; or shape into log, refrigerate, then slice. May be rolled in powdered sugar, small chocolate chips, or chopped peanuts. Store in air-tight container and refrigerate.

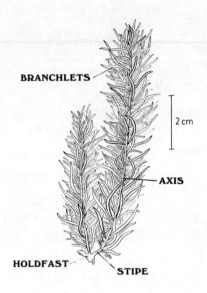

BRANCHLETS

2 cm

AXIS

HOLDFAST

STIPE

Analipus japonicus
(An-a-lee'-pus; fir needle or matsumo)

This seaweed was formerly classified as Heterochordaria abientina.

Description
Color: Light tan to deep olive to dark brown to green
Size: 6 to 10 inches long
Features: Short, slightly flattened, sometimes hollow branches resembling a spray of fir needles. Several *Analipus* may arise from the crustose holdfast.

Habitat & Distribution
Coastal Area: From Alaska to Central California
Tidal Conditions: Mid to low tide zones, found on rocks on moderately exposed shores

Foraging
Season: Late spring to autumn
Instructions: Cut or pull from rock

Preparation
Shelf-life: Short
Preservation: Dried. In Japan it is preboiled before drying to rid it of bitter flavor.

Uses
Tasty addition to soups and stir fries. In Japan it is sundried, salted, and cooked with soy sauce, or salted and made into sheets. Salted matsumo is also preserved and packed with alternate layers of edible mushrooms which have been washed in salt water.

Nutrients
High in protein, unsaturated fatty acids, and calcium. Also has polysaccharides and starch-like substances, iron, sodium, phosphorous, magnesium, molybdenum, selenium, and trace elements. Has high potency for lowering blood cholesterol levels. Is especially high in laminine, a basic amino acid which is effective against hypertension. Analipine, a peptide consisting of glutamic acid and aspartic acid has been isolated from *Analipus*. It is also reported to contain a great amount of thyroxin (thyroid hormone).

Analipus japonicus

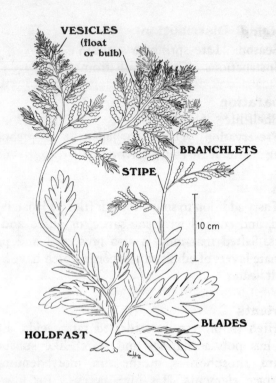

VESICLES
(float
or bulb)

BRANCHLETS

STIPE

10 cm

BLADES

HOLDFAST

Cystoseira
(sis tow si′ rus; chain bladder)

Related to the Sargassum group, two species of chain bladder occur on the West Coast, Cystoseira osmundacea and Cystoseira geminata.

Description
Color: Yellowish to dark brown
Size: *C. osmundacea*, reaches over 20 feet in length; *C. geminata*, 6 – 15 feet in length
Features: Strong cylindrical holdfast, woody stipe, numerous filiform branches which bear secondary branches and small air bladders that are born in pairs or chains. Tipmost float is pointed. In *C. osmundacea*, tough basal leaves resemble oak leaves; in *C. geminata*, basal leaves are narrow and resemble *Fucus*.

Habitat & Distribution

Coastal States: *C. osmundacea*-Oregon to Southern California; *C. geminata*-Alaska to Washington

Tidal Condition: Lower intertidal and subtidal zones

Foraging

Season: Spring, summer and early autumn

Instructions: Cut off tender portions of branches and blades. Although difficult to reach in lower intertidal areas, pieces of the chain bladder may be pulled loose.

Uses

Similar to *Sargassum*.

Nutrition

No information is available.

Cystoseira

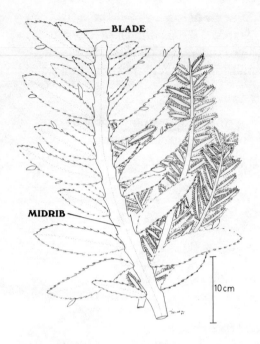

BLADE

MIDRIB

10 cm

Desmarestia ligulata
(dez mar es' tia; color changer)

At one time, this species had several different names, but now Desmarestia ligulata includes all regional forms which have flattened blades and midribs. There are several other species of Desmarestia in east and west coastal waters.

Description

Color: Light brown to chocolate brown, turning green when taken from water.

Size: 1½ - 1¼ feet (40 - 60 cm) long, and 8 - 16 inches (20 - 40 cm) wide; but may reach over 3 feet in length and 36 inches wide.

Features: Holdfast measures up to 1½ inches (4 cm). Stipe cylindrical at base, flattened at blade. Numerous branches. Central flattened axial blade, 1 - 2 inches (2.5 - 5 cm) wide.

Desmarestia (color changer)

Habitat & Distribution

Coastal States: Alaska to Mexico, also in the Atlantic

Tidal Condition: Lowest part of intertidal and subtidal zones

Foraging

Instructions: Often found cast up in heaps. Avoid collecting with other plants or animals, as the cell sap of *Desmarestia ligulata* contains sulfuric acid, which is released when the plant is damaged or handled. The strong acid quickly bleaches and digests plants and animals it contacts.

Preparation: Gather from rocks – keep separate from other plants and animals. Not ordinarily used or preserved – has high surfuric acid content.

Uses

The plant is generally not recommended as suitable for eating. A novel method of extracting the strong acid, used to make pickles, is presented below.

Desmarestia Vinegar

Desmarestia species contain sulfuric acid, which is certainly rare if not unique in the plant kingdom. The following method will give a very strong acid extract with a pH of 1.2; which is considerably more acid than ordinary vinegar's pH of 1.9, commonly used in pickle recipes. This recipe is quite new and the effects of *Desmarestia* on the body are unknown. However, we have tasted it without ill effect.

Simmer 9 quarts *Desmaretia* in 1 quart water 20 to 30 minutes. Strain in collander. Makes about 1¾ quarts liquid to use in pickle recipes.

Desmarestia-Nereocystis Sour Pickles

For the more daring.

Pack into jars 3 quarts *Nereocystis* slices. To 1¾ quarts *Desmarestia* extract, prepared as above, add 5 tablespoons salt and bring to boil. To each jar of *Nereocystis* add 1 teaspoon pickling spice, 1 teaspoon dill or flower of dill, and one clove garlic. Fill to ½ inch of top with boiling *Desmarestia*-salt mixture, seal and process 10 minutes in boiling water bath. Allow to ripen 1 week or longer.

Note: If these pickles seem a bit too salty and sour, I suggest experimenting with other recipes, too.

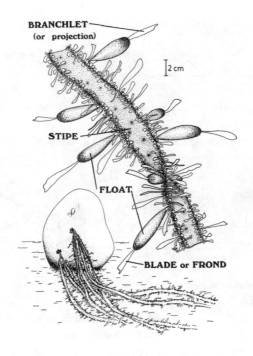

Egregia menziesii
(eh gree' jah; feather boa or boa kelp)

Description
Color: Dark brown to olive green
Size: Up to 11 feet (10m) in length
Features: Sturdy holdfast, repeated and somewhat irregular stipe branches. Stipe is cylindrical near the base, somewhat flattened, broad (4 to 6 inches) and bladelike near the tip. Thick, tough, rough texture. Bears a number of blunt projections, small blades ½ inches (1 to 2 cm.) wide, and small oblong floats or bladders from each blade.

Habitat & Distribution
Coastal Area: British Columbia to California
Tidal Condition: Lower intertidal to subtidal zones,

Egregia (feather boa)

attached to rocks in moderately exposed waters; in the higher intertidal regions, it is found on more exposed shores.

Foraging

Season: Spring to autumn

Instructions: Pluck or cut tender parts of young plants and floats or bladders. Older, large plants are tough, so only use the bladder. Use fresh, not easily preserved.

Uses

Although *Egregia* is thick and tough, the plant becomes tender with brief cooking. The floats make an interesting and attractive additions to soups, stews and stir fries. *Egregia* has been used, along with other large kelps, as a mulch and fertilizer by coastal farmers.

Nutrition

No information available.

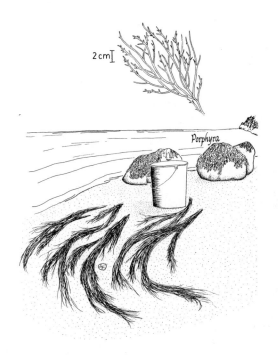

Gracilaria verrucosa & G. sjoestedtii
(gras sa lar' iah; "ogo" in Hawaii)

Description
Color: Usually reddish brown to reddish purple, sometimes pale or yellowish

Size: Up to 6 feet (2m) long and 1/16 inch (2mm) wide

Features: Branched, spaghetti-like strings, grow in clusters from small holdfasts, usually attached to shells or wood pieces under sand. Irregular, sometimes proliferous branching. Cylindrical in shape. Cartilaginous texture. Delicious fragrance. When dried, it has a horny texture, resembling coarse dark hair.

Habitat & Distribution
Coastal Area: From the Arctic to the Tropics; both coasts

Tidal Condition: Lower intertidal regions, quiet bays, and protected, slightly brackish locations

Foraging

Season: Late spring and summer

Instructions: Found on rocks and shells in sandy areas or washed up to shore in large piles. Often requires some washing (preferably in saltwater, then rinsed quickly in freshwater) and picking over to remove extraneous material. May be used fresh. May be frozen unrinsed, (or rinse in clean seawater) also may be blanched and frozen. May be pickled.

Uses

Gracilaria is an important commercial source of agar; it may also be used for homemade agar. Various species are also used for making *Gracilaria* gum. *Gracilaria* is a very popular sea vegetable in Hawaii, where it is used fresh, blanched, or salted; in salads, relishes and pickles. It may also be cooked and used to thicken stews. *Gracilaria* is artificially cultured in the Orient.

Nutrition

Gracilaria is medium in protein, high in manganese, and contains nitrogen, potassium, zinc, and vitamins A and B. Also it contains agar, sugar, fat, sulfur, iodine, calcium, iron, chloride, silicon, and trace elements.

Recipes follow. See also *Postelsia*, Sea Palm and Ogo Salad.

Gracilaria Kombu Soup

4 cups water
1 ten inch piece kombu cut in pieces
    (use dried *Laminaria* or *Alaria*)
1 tomato, diced

½ onion, diced
¼ cup miso (soybean paste)
3 to 4 slices cheese, diced
1 cup *Gracilaria* cut in 4 inch pieces

Bring water to boil with kombu and onions. Simmer 10 minutes. Add miso and tomato and cheese, continue simmering 5 minutes. Add *Gracilaria* and serve immediately.

Gracilaria Spaghetti and Tomato Sauce

May be made with or without meat.

1 tablespoon oil (olive preferably)
½ pound ground beef
1 medium onion, chopped
1 clove minced garlic
⅛ teaspoon cayenne
1 can tomato sauce, 8 ounce
¼ cup grated carrot
2 cups *Gracilaria*
2 quarts boiling water
½ cup cheese, grated (opt.)

Brown meat in oil with onion and garlic. Add tomato sauce, cayenne, carrot, and herbs and simmer 15 minutes. Drop *Gracilaria* into the boiling water for just 15 seconds. Drain; serve with sauce and top with grated cheese.

Guacamole Sandwich Spread or Dip

1 avocado, mashed (about half a cup)
1 tomato, diced (about half a cup)

½ cup fresh *Gracilaria*, washed and chopped
juice of half a lemon
⅛ teaspoon cayenne or piece of chili pepper, chopped
¼ cup chopped sweet onion or green onions
¼ cup cream cheese or jack cheese pieces

Blend lemon juice and mashed avocado. Add remaining ingredients and serve on toasted buns, crackers or corn chips.

Gracilaria Salad (a la Hawaii)

2 cups fresh *Gracilaria*, chopped (may be steamed briefly and cooled first if desired)
½ pound cottage cheese
4 radishes, grated
2 tomatoes, sliced
½ cup green onions, chopped

Arrange *Gracilaria* on bottom of serving plate. Mix cottage cheese and grated radishes and place in middle. Sprinkle with onions. Arrange tomato slices around outside. Serve with yogurt dressing below.

Yogurt Dressing:
½ cup yogurt
½ cup mayonnaise
1 clove garlic, grated
1 teaspoon combination of spices: tarragon, thyme, marjoram, *Porphyra* flour, kelp powder, parsley, dill and basil. (See recipe for *Porphyra* Salad Seasonings.)

Gracilaria Relish

"Ogo namasu," a recipe from Hawaii.

	Marinade:
2 cups *Gracilaria*	¼ cup vegetable oil
½ tomato	¼ cup cider vinegar
½ cup sweet red onion	3 tablespoons shoyu
1 cucumber (opt.)	1 tablespoon sugar
1 clove garlic grated	½ teaspoon salt
	½ teaspoon fresh ginger, grated
	pinch cayenne

Wilt the *Gracilaria* by steaming very briefly over boiling water. Rinse immediately under cold water. Cut into 2 to 3 inch sections. Cut the tomato, onion and cucumber into small pieces or strips. Add the *Gracilaria* and combine with the marinade. Chill. Let stand 2 hours before serving.

Ogo Kim Chee (Pickled Gracilaria)

Very popular in Korea.

2 pounds fresh *Gracilaria*, chopped into 2 or 3 inch pieces (about 2 quarts)
½ cup salt
2 cloves garlic, chopped
1 small bunch green onions, or 1 or 2 onions chopped
2 small red chillies
1 piece of ginger root, very finely chopped or grated (1 teaspoon)

Wash and clean the *Gracilaria*. Place in crock or china bowl, sprinkle with salt and mix well. Weigh down with heavy plate, and let stand over night. Rinse well, add other ingredients, mix, pack tightly into jars and keep cool. Allow to ferment two days till tart and red in color. Refrigerate. Let stand a few days before using.

Party Dip Hawaiian

1 cup Ogo Kim Chee (see above)
1 package softened cream cheese, 8 ounce
1 tablespoon mayonnaise

Put cream cheese in bowl and mix in mayonnaise. Chop Kim Chee finely and add to cheese mixture. This improves upon sitting at room temperature for a few hours and also keeps well in refrigerator. Can be used with chips, crackers, etc., or served on toast.

Sunomono

1 cup fresh *Gracilaria*
boiling water

Clean and wash the *Gracilaria*. Blanch by placing it in a colander and pouring boiling water over it (turns green). Chill and serve with one of the dressings below.

Dressing I
½ cup vinegar
1 tablespoon honey
salt

Dressing II
¼ cup lemon juice
2 tablespoons honey
salt

Dressing III
¼ cup vinegar
1 teaspoon soy sauce
1 tablespoon honey
salt

Dressing IV
¼ cup miso
2 tablespoons rice or cider vinegar
2 tablespoons honey
salt

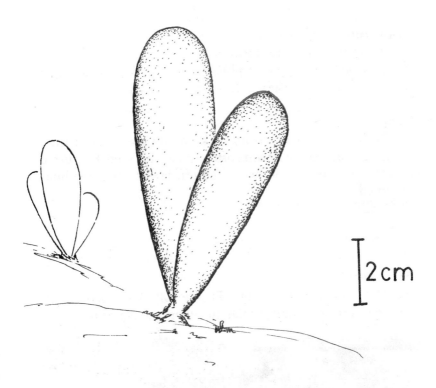

2 cm

Halosaccion glandiforme
(hal o sac' ee on; sea sac)

Description
Color: Yellowish-green to yellowish-brown, to reddish-purple

Size: Up to 10 inches (26 cm) long and 1 inch (2.5 cm) in diameter

Features: Hollow, thin-walled, elongated sacs; the sac contains water, but near the top it is gas-filled; grows profusely, several plants from a single holdfast

Habitat & Distribution
Coastal Area: Alaska to Mexico

Tidal Condition: Mid intertidal zone; found on rocks in exposed and sheltered areas

Foraging

Season: Spring to autumn

Instructions: May be plucked from rocks, or the larger plants snipped off to leave developing smaller ones in place.

Preparation

Note: Pull or cut from rock; young plants need little cleaning; older, eroded plants often filled with sand. Encrusted holdfast portion should be trimed off. Preservation methods not tried.

Uses

Used fresh or in soups, etc.

Nutrients

Not much information. Presumably has food value, minerals and vitamins similar to other sea vegetables.

Halosaccion glandiforme (sea sac)

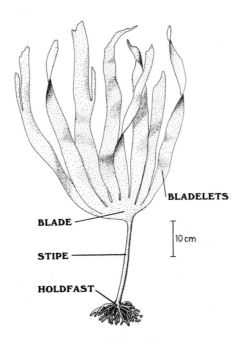

Laminaria
(lam in air' ee yah; kelp or kombu)

There are several species on the West Coast.

Description
Color: Olive green to dark brown
Size: Large; one to several feet (⅓ to 2m) in length
Features: Texture varies from thin and tender to thick and leathery, depending on species and age. Branched holdfast. Strong, flexible stipe. Narrow and straplike to broad, fan-shaped, divided or corrugated blade, depending on the species. Many *Lamanaria* serve as sources of the important colloid, alginate, widely used in a number of industries. They contain taste enhancing sodium glutamate. *L. saccharina,* called sugar wrack, is sweet, owing to the presence of mannitol, a sugar alcohol.

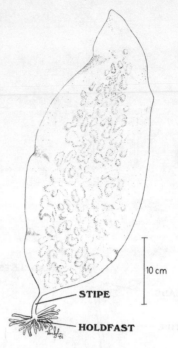

STIPE

HOLDFAST

Young L. saccharina plant.

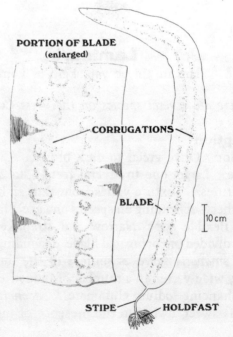

PORTION OF BLADE
(enlarged)

CORRUGATIONS

BLADE

STIPE   HOLDFAST

Laminaria saccharina plant.

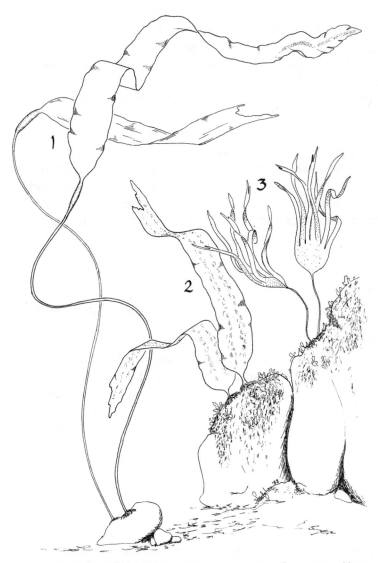

1. **Laminaria longicrurus, 2. L. agardhii,
3. L. digitata.**

Habitat & Distribution

Coastal Area: Alaska to California

Tidal Condition: Lower intertidal, usually attached to rocks, in cool water currents. The species *L. saccharina* is found growing on shells, wood and rocks in moderately to very sheltered waters between lower and subtidal regions. This species ranges from the Aleutians to Coos Bay, Oregon.

There are several Atlantic species of *Laminaria*. Horsetail kelp, tangle, and finger kelp. *L. digitata* resembles *L. setchellii,* or *L. dentigera* (illustrated), and occurs in the low intertidal and subtidal zones from the Arctic to Long Island Sound, and subtidally southward. Hollowstem kelp, *L. longicruris,* and common southern kelp, *L. agardhii* are very long and straplike, occurring from Long Island Sound and off New York harbor to the Gulf of Maine, and in the Arctic.

Foraging

Season: Late spring to autumn

Instructions: Cut the strong stipe from rock with knife

Preparation

Preservation: Sundried or partially-dried, folded and pressed while pliable, and slivered across the grain for use in soups. Dried plants are hydrated by soaking 30 minutes in water before dropped into soups or used to roll around stuffings. East Coast foragers may substitute *Laminaria* stipes in the *Nereocystis pickle recipes.*

Note: *Laminaria* is often used in pharmaceuticals; see Chapter 10, Seaweeds in the Medicine Chest. It is also used in making glue and seaweed meal.

Nutrients

Laminaria species are high in iodine, calcium and potassium. They also contain alginic acid (15-40%), laminaran (18-33%), mannitol (5-36%), fucoidan (5-20%), D-glucose, D-galactose, protein (5-12%), carotene, niacin, phosphorus, sodium, the B complex vitamins, vitamin C, and many other elements. See Table 5, p. 62 for an analysis of the Japanese species of *Laminaria*.

The content of mannitol, a sugar alcohol, fluctuates with the season, and depth to which the algae grow. *Laminaria saccharina* fronds contain about 5% in January and up to 22% in May. Mannitol, which is sweet tasting, is used in the production of tablets for diabetic foods, for making chewing gum, and as a dusting powder.

Laminaran, a reserve carbohydrate comparable to starch in higher plants, is found in highest concentration in autumn and early winter. The content declines with depth. There are several medical uses of laminaran sulfate.

Alginic acid is an acid membrane mucilage typical of brown algae. The content of alginic acid fluctuates greatly with the season and depth.

Protein content is highest in March.

Recipes follow.

Kelp Powder or Flakes

Make from any of the several species of Laminaria, or other brown sea vegetables such as Alaria or Macrocystis.

Wash gathered *Laminaria* in fresh water quickly to remove sand and shells. Spread and dry in sun and breeze. Heat dried *Laminaria* fronds in slow oven, (about 200 to 250 degrees) 10 minutes or until they turn green and crisp. Remove and pulverize in blender or with mortar and pestle. Store in jar for use as seasoning on the table, in place of salt, or use in recipes.

Kelp powder contains a concentrated mix of minerals, which although salty, is preferable to table salt (sodium chloride), especially for salt restricted diets, because of its high proportion of potassium to sodium, and because of the many other important minerals and vitamins it provides. Kelp powder enhances the flavors of foods. It dissolves better when slightly heated. A coarse ground powder, or small flakes are fine for soups.

Crunchy Kelp

Fry small pieces of dried *Laminaria* in oil, turning them until the color changes to green. Keep moderate temperature and watch so it doesn't burn. Drain on absorbant paper and serve immediately. May crumble over cooked grains or potatoes; or serve on popcorn with brewer's yeast or favorite herb seasonings.

Kombu Stock

The most important use of Laminaria in Japanese cooking.

For 1 to 2 ounces kombu use 1 to 1½ quarts of water in saucepan. Let stand 30 to 60 minutes. Slowly heat to almost boiling, but do not allow to boil. Remove kombu.

The traditional Japanese stock usually also contains dried bonito flakes – ⅓ to 1 ounce bonito flakes are added to stock after the kombu is removed. The broth is brought to a boil, and then strained through a cloth.

Kombu, featured in many Japanese recipes, was the only source of stock allowed to Buddhist priests, who were forbidden to eat meat. The natural monosodium glutamate is the source of the pleasing flavor of kombu stock. Care must be taken not to boil the kombu, as higher temperatures release bitter flavors, and dissolve polysaccharides, making the soup sticky.

Pan-Fry Fish or Vegetables

Use 1 pound summer squash, zucchini, or fish fillets.

3 tablespoons fine cornmeal
1 tablespoon kelp powder, or kelp flakes (see instructions for
    making this from species of *Laminaria* or use purchased
    kelp powder
2 teaspoons thyme
1 teaspoon Spike, or other Italian seasonings (opt.)
¼ cup oil

Cut vegetables in slices or wedges. Heat oil in skillet.
Combine cornmeal, kelp powder and seasonings in shallow
bowl. Press vegetable pieces or fish fillets into mixture, coating
thoroughly. Fry until golden brown. Serve hot.

Kelp Powder Vegetable Soup

Makes four servings.

1½ quarts water
2 cups vegetable greens, such as broccoli, kale, parsley stems,
    celery, etc. or other left-over greens or trimmings
½ cup onions, diced
1 cup carrots, sliced
1 cup potatoes, diced
1 small bay leaf
1 teaspoon cumin
2 teaspoons mineral seasonings, Spike, or mixture of herbs,
    such as thyme, marjoram, oregano, etc.
1 to 2 teaspoons kelp powder or flakes (may use more)
3 tablespoons tamari (soy sauce)
4 tablespoons chopped parsley for garnish, or sprinkle each
    serving with ½ teaspoon dried parsley flakes

Combine all ingredients except chopped parsley. Simmer 2 to 3 hours. Remove vegetables if clear soup is desired. Ladle into bowls and garnish with parsley.

Kelp Lentil Soup

2 quarts water
2 cups lentils
1 piece kombu (dried *Laminaria* or *Alaria*)
2 onions, chopped
1 clove garlic, minced and crushed
2 to 3 potatoes, scrubbed and diced into large cubes
1 carrot, diced
1 stalk celery, chopped
5 leaves fresh sage, minced
1 bay leaf
dash cayenne
½ to 1 teaspoon oregano
3 or 4 fronds dried *Porphyra* (or use fresh if available)

While the water is heating up, add the seaweed and let it reconstitute (a minute or two). Remove and cut into pieces (large is fine). Return to pot. Add lentils, vegetables, and herbs. Bring to boil, reduce heat to low and simmer for 1½ to 2 hours, or until lentils and *Porphyra* are tender.

Note: A pressure cooker may be used. Cover and bring to 15 pounds pressure. Cook for about 35 minutes. Cool. Add salt or miso to taste.

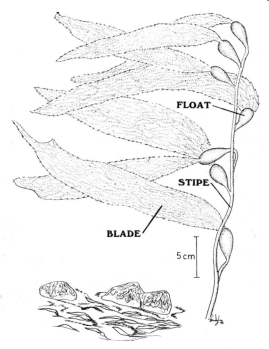

FLOAT

STIPE

BLADE

5 cm

Macrocystis integrifolia & M. pyrifera
(mac ro sis' tus; small, and giant perennial kelp)

Description

Color: Golden brown to rich deep brown

Size: 100 to 200 feet (30m to 60m) or longer in California, but much shorter in Washington. Blades are 9 to 12 inches (25 to 35cm) long, 2 inches (5cm) wide.

Features: The giant kelp forms huge beds off the California coast. A perennial, the plant lives 7 to 8 years, held to the substrate in deep water by a huge branched rhyzomelike holdfast. The cylindrical stipe branches into a number of long unequal parts. At intervals blades arise. At the base of each blade is a gas-filled float. Hundreds of such blade-bearing floats may be borne on a single, repeatedly branched stipe. These floats buoy up the kelp into the upper waters, where light penetrates. The blades have an irregularly corrugated shiny surface and sharply toothed margins.

Habitat & Distribution

Coastal Area: *M. pyrifera* – California coast. *M. integrifolia* – full length of North and South America from Alaska to the Strait of Juan de Fuca.

Tidal Conditions: *M. pyrifera* – occurs in deeper waters, lowest portion of the intertidal and subtidal waters. *M. integrifolia* – lowest portion of the intertidal and subtidal waters. Favors cold temperate waters and areas exposed to the open sea but somewhat sheltered from the full force of heavy wave action.

Foraging

Season: A perennial, *Macrocystis* occurs throughout the year. Sometimes found in good condition cast up on the shore.

Instructions: Portions of plant can be reached at low tide in a few locations, or harvested by diving, or from a boat, using a knife to cut.

Preparation and Use

Macrocystis may be dried and pulverized to make kelp powder. Use the smaller species, *M. integrifolia* in many recipes. Very tasty cooked; sliced hollow bladders are a great addition to soups, stews and stir fries, or as topping for pizza.

Macrocystis (perennial kelp)

Also may be pickled. Commercial exploitation is carried out on a large scale for the production of the phycocolloid, algin, and it is also dried and pulverized for kelp tablets sold as diet supplements and as a salt substitute.

Several important drugs derived from *Macrocystis* have been developed and marketed. See Chapter Nine, Seaweeds in the Medicine Chest.

Nutrients

High in vitamin E, A, B complex and D. Also contains iodine, and vitamin C. The average ash content of *Macrocystis* is 39.4% and includes principally potassium, sodium, calcium, magnesium, and phosphorus. Minor elements are strontium, iron, boron, aluminum, barium and zinc. Trace elements are chromium, manganese, copper, cadmium, lead, cobalt and mercury. Alginic acid range is 14–21%. It also contains laminaran, fucoidan and mannitol. (See discussion under *Laminaria.*)

Korean Pepper Soup

1 stewing chicken
1 cup thinly sliced *Macrocystis* fronds and bulbs
1 clove garlic, grated
2 green onions, chopped
2 to 3 tablespoons shoyu to taste
1 to 2 teaspoons black pepper, or less for milder taste

Cover chicken with water in large pot, and cook until tender. Remove chicken and use in another dish. To each 4 cups broth, add amount listed of remaining ingredients.

Note: Other seaweeds may be substituted such as *Alaria, Gracilaria, Nereocystis,* or *Cystoseira* in place of *Macrocystis. Cystoseira* is said to be especially delicious. Some have recommended *Odonthalia.*

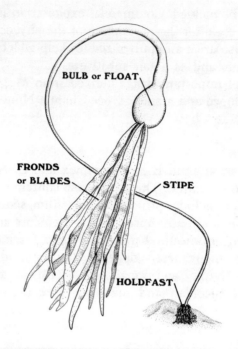

BULB or FLOAT

FRONDS or BLADES

STIPE

HOLDFAST

Nereocystis luetkeana

(Neer ee o sis' tus; bull kelp, bullwhip kelp, or ribbon kelp)

Description

Color: Olive green to dark brown

Size: To 100 feet (30m) long

Features: An annual; stout holdfast; hollow stipe reaching to 75 or more feet long, terminating in an enlarged spherical float which contains carbon monoxide. Profusion of long blades, 9 to 12 feet (3 to 4m) long, 5 inches (13cm) wide, which trail in the water.

Habitat & Distribution

Coastal area: Alaska to California

Tidal Condition: Low intertidal and subtidal zones to depths of 30 feet or more in areas with rocky bottoms.

Foraging
Season: Spring and summer.
Instructions: Usually, *Nereocystis* may be reached only at low tides. Wading or a boat may be required. Cast-up plants occasionally are found fresh. Unless the stipe and bulb are going to be used, the blades alone may be partially cropped, leaving most of the plant intact for further growth.

Preparation
Preservation: Dry and freeze young blades. Older blades may be strong tasting due to the high potassium content.

Uses
Small to medium-sized, or even large-sized bull kelp bulbs and stipes become tender with brief cooking, and may be prepared in a number of ways. East Coast foragers may substitute *Laminaria* stipes. Older *Nereocystis* plants often bear epiphytic seaweeds (growing attached to the stipe or bulb). One of these is a choice nori, *Porphyra nereocystis*. Another is a delicate red seaweed, *Antithamnionella pacifica,* which is beautiful pressed on note cards (Chapter Eleven).

The unique structure of *Nereocystis* lent itself to many creative uses by Pacific Northwest Coastal Indians. They used the bulb and stipe as containers, and the dried stipe as fishing gear. It was also used in such recreational activities as targets for throwing, and amunition for blow guns. It is said that Natives Americans of Sitka, Alaska, used it like a teakettle to cure headache. Steam was generated by heating the bulb, and conducted via the small end of the hollow stipe to the ear. We can imagine that Indians might have used them for jump ropes, as we do today. Lengths of stipe were also used as water conduits.

For use as containers, bulb and stipe were cured by soaking in fresh water and then dried. Liquids such a grease rendered from eulachon (candlefish), oil from smelt, melted deer suet, water and even molasses was poured into the float or length of stipe with one end tied. The ends were sealed by

Sons Ted and John rendering bullwhip kelp horn requiem for beached sperm whales near Florence, Oregon.

tying, and the stipe coiled for storage in chests, or hung. To use the liquid they simply untied the knot, squeezed out the desired quantity, and retied it, for further storage.

For fishing gear, the long rope-like stipes, dried and cured, were spliced or plaited together for use as fishing and harpoon lines, nets and ropes. Kelp lines were dried for storage, and soaked in water before use to restore flexibility. The bulb was also used as a mold to fashion fishing hooks from Douglas fir and hemlock knots, and shape the ends of their bows made from yew.

A special delicacy in their diets, the blades on which herring had spawned were served with oil rendered from eulachon or smelt. Sundried and stored in boxes for the winter, the seaweed was preserved, and then soaked overnight and boiled before serving.

Alaskan Indians and Eskimos report preparing a brew called hoochinoo from *Nereocystis*. Seatron, a reputably delectable product, is prepared by removing the salt, adding flavorings and candying portions of the stipes and bulbs, still sells in the Northwest.

Nutrients

Nereocystis luetkeana (bullwhip, or bull kelp) harvested near Vashon Island in Puget Sound in May 1978, was analyzed by scientists at the Department of Food Science and Technology of Washington State University. It was found to contain relatively high amounts of protein, minerals and carbohydrates, while remaining low in fat. One hundred grams of freeze-dried bull kelp contributes significant quantities of the essential elements calcium (51% of the adult daily requirement), iron (43%) and zinc (18.6%). The frond portion contains a very high amount of protein (15.3%) which is of high quality, comparable to lean beef and whole cooked eggs based on the amino acid composition. The stipe and bulb contain about half as much protein as the fronds (7.3% and 6.4%), while crude fiber is nearly five times greater in the stipe than in the frond. Other studies of this sea vegetable show a protein content of the fronds ranging from 11 to 15% over the growing season (April to October).

Bullwhip kelp is high in potassium, sodium, iodine and magnesium, and contains bromine, sulfur, phosphorus, silicon and trace elements. Unfortunately, plants tested from Vashon Island in Puget Sound, which receives pollution from smelters and other sources, contained rather high levels of arsenic, strontium and barium.

Nereocystis, valuable as a fertilizer, a mineral and vitamin supplement to animal feed, and a source of potassium and iodine, contains an excellent commercial source of the colloid algin (alginate), and for this purpose is harvested in California.

Recipes follow.

Table 7

Vashon Island Bull Kelp Nutrients

Nutrient	U.S. R.D.A	% R.D.A. In 100g Frond.	% R.D.A. In 100g Stipe.
Protein	65 g	23.3	11.3
Calcium	1000 mg	51.0	65.0
Iron	18 mg	43.3	17.2
Zinc	15 mg	18.6	8.3

Per 100 grams	Frond	Stipe
Total Calories	233.8	215.0
Carbohydrate	38.8g	41.0g
Fat	2.0g	2.4g
Protein	15.3g	7.3g

Information from E. S. Barta, L. S. Branen and H. K. Leung.

Table 8

California Bull Kelp Nutrients

Nutrient	U.S. R.D.A.	Per Serving ½ ounce (14.2g)	% R.D.A. Per Serving
Protein, g	65.	1.7	2.6
Fat, g		0.18	
Carbohydrates, g		5.09	
Calories		28.	
Vitamin A, I.U.	5000.	1376.	27.5
Vitamin C, mg	60.	2.47	4.1
Thiamine, mg	1.5	0.065	4.3
Riboflavin, mg	1.7	0.183	10.8
Niacin, mg	20.	0.554	2.8
Calcium, mg	1000.	177.	8.8
Iron, mg	18.	0.56	3.1
Phosphorus, mg	1000.	59.	5.9
Magnesium, mg	400.	78.	19.5
Copper, mg		0.08	.08
Zinc, mg		0.19	1.3
Sodium, mg		653.	
Potassium, mg		2300.	

Information from Matthew Hodel of Ocean Energy, Soquel, California. Analysis by ANRESCO, Inc.

Pickle - O - Relish

4½ quarts sliced bullwhip kelp
2 cups chopped onions
2 small hot peppers, chopped
1 cup chopped sweet red peppers
2 cloves garlic, sliced
boiling water
¾ cups sugar or ½ cup honey
4 cups vinegar
2 cups water
2 tablespoons pickling spices
2 teaspoons salt

Slice kelp into rings. Cover kelp, onions and peppers with boiling water. Let stand 5 minutes. Drain. Repeat. Cover third time with boiling water. Let stand 10 minutes. Drain.

Tie spices in bag. Combine all ingredients in large pot. Heat to nearly boiling. Simmer 10 minutes. Remove spices. Bring to boiling, and pack into clean hot jars. Fill with boiling liquid to about ¼ inch from top. Screw down sealing lid, and if desired, process five minutes in boiling water bath, for preserving.

Nereocystis Dill Pickles

Not too sour nor too salty, and they keep well. The best I've tasted.

Gather fresh *Nereocystis*. Remove blades and wash stipes. Cut into lengths or slices to fit jars. Depending on the size of the *Nereocystis* it will take five to ten plants.

Pack the lengths of *Nereocystis* stipes closely, fitting smaller sections into larger ones. Add a washed grape leaf, a dill head, and if desired, a garlic clove, ½ teaspoon pickling spices, a chili, or dash of cayenne for each quart. Fill with boiling brine to ½ inch from top of jar.

Temper the filled jars by placing in tub of hot water before placing in water bath to avoid breaking. Screw down lid and process in boiling water bath for 15 minutes for quarts, or 25 minutes for gallons.

I have made pickles without processing in the hot water bath and they have kept fine. They are much firmer if not cooked, but may keep better if processed. Also, the spices may be omitted if a more bland product is desired, for instance, to use as topping on a pizza.

Nereocystis Dill Pickles # 1

2 quarts vinegar (should test 5-6% acid)
4 quarts water
4 to 6 tablespoons pickling salt
½ teaspoon alum (not needed with grape leaves)
dill heads, one for each quart
clove garlic for each quart

Prepare and process as in recipe above. Makes 3 gallons.

Nereocystis Dill Pickles # 2

¼ cup pickling salt
2¾ cups vinegar
3 cups water
5 to 6 peppercorns, 1 dill head, 1 grape leaf, and 1 clove garlic per quart

Prepare and process as in recipe above. Makes 3 quarts.

Nereocystis Cold Pickles

A means of preserving Nereocystis for later use.

1 gallon vinegar (white prefered)
½ cup salt
3 cups sugar or 1½ cups honey
1 cup finely diced horseraddish, or several chillies
1 clove garlic (opt.)

Place slices or chunks of *Nereocystis* stipes and bulbs in containers. Large jars or crocks may be used. Pour vinegar mixture over them and permit to ripen several days before serving. To preserve *Nereocystis* for use in recipes, such as *Nereocystis* pizza, omit horseradish and chillies. Soak these pickles first in water to remove some of the sour taste. *Nereocystis* bulbs preserved this way may also be stuffed like green peppers.

Favorite Sweet Pickles

2 quarts of hollow bulbs and stipes cut about ½ inches long
2 cups sugar or 1½ cups honey
2 teaspoons each of celery seed, turmeric, mustard seed and pickling spice
1 medium onion sliced
1 teaspoon salt
1 clove garlic or ¼ teaspoon powdered garlic
1½ cups white vinegar

Combine all ingredients and let stand three hours. Heat to boiling and seal in hot jars. Needs no further processing. This is a very easy method, and gives an excellent product.
 If a more tart pickle is desired, decrease sugar to 1 cup.

Sweet-Sour Dill Rings

Great for topping pizza!

4 quarts *Nereocystis* stipe cut into rings
2 celery stalks, quartered (opt.)
8 heads fresh dill
4 cups sugar or 2½ cups honey
½ cup salt
1 quart vinegar
2 cups water
2 onions, sliced

Rinse freshly harvested *Nereocystis* stipes and cut into ¼ inch rings. To each sterilized quart jar add 3 or 4 slices onion, 2 pieces celery and 2 heads dill.

Dissolve sugar and salt in vinegar and water; bring to boil. Pack seaweed slices into jars. Pour vinegar solution, while hot, over *Nereocystis* in each jar to cover; seal at once. Store in cool place. For best flavor, do not use for 3 to 4 weeks. Makes 4 quarts.

Stuffed Nereocystis Hors D'Oeuvres

For these attractive circles of Nereocystis, stuffed with a variety of colorful fillings, use recipe for Nereocystis Dills. Stuff lengths with one of the fillings below, and slice into ¼ inch rings and serve alone, or on small rounds of toast or crackers. Fillings may also be spread on bread or crackers and topped with a pickle ring.

Circles stuffed with cream cheese.

Use plain cream cheese, or any of the flavored spreads, such as chive or pimiento cream cheese, or a colorful port wine cheddar spread. Fill pickled *Nereocystis* tube with the cheese which has been softened at room temperature. Slice.

Circles stuffed with wieners.

Select pickled *Nereocystis* stipe lengths which are the right size for stuffing with a wiener. Insert the wiener and slice into circles.

Circles stuffed with cheese.

Grate cheddar, jack cheese, or Swiss cheese with medium fine grater. If desired add small amount of tomato paste for color. Spike and cayenne are also good additions to add more zip. Fill lengths of pickled *Nereocystis* stipe and slice.

Circles with Tofu-Nut Butter Spread.

Combine ¼ cup peanut butter, ½ cup tofu and 1 tablespoon miso or barley. Mash and blend with fork. Ground sunflower seeds or raisins may also be added. Stuff *Nereocystis* and slice. Substitute tahini for peanut butter for a variation.

Circles stuffed with Split Pea Spread.

Combine 1 cup cooked, drained yellow split peas with 2 tablespoons mayonnaise, 1 pound tofu, 1 cup ground toasted sunflower or sesame seeds, ½ teaspoon turmeric, 1 teaspoon salt and dash of soy sauce. Mash and mix thoroughly. Fill pickled *Nereocystis* lengths and slice into rings. Substitute 2 tablespoons parmesan cheese and 2 tablespoons cottage cheese for the tofu for a variation. Add basil or spike and a dash of pepper.

Guess-Again Salad

Some think it's chicken, others potatoes, but it's really tempeh, the miracle high protein soy food invented in Indonesia, combined with nutritious Nereocystis Dill Pickles. But whatever you decide to call it, it's scrumptious.

6 ounce tempeh
⅓ cup Yogurt and Mayonnaise dressing (see recipe)
1 stalk celery, chopped
¼ cup diced onion or ½ cup sliced green onions
1 cup *Nereocystis* dill pickle rings
1 teaspoon prepared mustard
1 teaspoon shoyu
½ teaspoon turmeric (opt.)

Steam tempeh 20 minutes over boiling water. Cool and cut into small cubes, about ½ inch. Combine with remaining ingredients and mix gently. Serve on greens as salad or mash for dip or sandwich filling.

Surfer Cider

Nereocystis fronds are definitely worth keeping, with 15% high quality protein, plus giant amounts of calcium, iron and vitamins. You can make this drink either from the fresh or dried fronds. Try other seaweeds also.

For each cup:
1 teaspoon dried *Nereocystis* fronds crushed to measure
    or ½ cup fresh fronds, cut into pieces
1 cup cider
½ teaspoon cinnamon or pumpkin pie spices
½ teaspoon honey or dash or lemon (opt.)

Place *Nereocystis* in pan with cider and bring slowly to simmer. Add cinnamon and honey or lemon. Blend in blender, strain if desired, cool and enjoy.

Bull and Mussel Salad

2 cups cooked mussels
1 cup strained mussel liquid from steaming mussels
1 carrot, peeled and sliced
2 onions, thinly sliced
2 cloves minced garlic
¼ teaspoon ground allspice
½ teaspoon each crumbled basil and tarragon
1 bay leaf
freshly ground pepper and/or cayenne, as desired
1 cup liquid from Nereocystis Dill Pickles
2 tablespoons olive oil
3 cups boiled, diced potatoes
1½ cups *Nereosystis* dill pickle rings
1 cup sour cream

Steam fresh mussels in large covered pot until they open (only a few minutes – don't overcook). Take mussels out of shell, remove any byssus threads and pearls. Measure 2 cups.

Combine cooked mussels with herbs, pickle juice, olive oil, onions, garlic and carrots in a non-metallic container. Marinate 24 hours (or less if you are in a hurry). Drain, combine with potatoes, pickles and sour cream. Garnish with marinaded vegetables and more *Nereocystis* pickle rings if desired.

Rings and Balls Stew

Uses about 1 medium Nereocystis plant.

2 to 3 tablespoons oil
1 onion
½ cup sliced mushrooms (optional)
2 cups *Nereocystis* fronds, chopped

3 cups slices of *Nereocystis* rings from bulb and stipe
3 cups cooked garbanzo beans
1 can whole tomatoes, 28 ounce
2 teaspoons each thyme and basil
1 teaspoon mixed salad seasonings or use Italian seasonings
¼ to ½ cup parmesan cheese for garnish

Sauté onions and mushrooms gently. Add *Nereocystis* fronds and rings and cook a few minutes until sea vegetables turn green. Add garbanzos and water in which they were cooked, and remaining ingredients, and cook gently about 15 minutes. Garnish with parmesan cheese.

Succotash

½ cup *Nereocystis* stipe slices
1 cup cooked lima beans
1 cup whole kernel corn
2 tablespoons chopped onion
1 clove garlic, grated
1 green pepper, sliced
1 teaspoon cumin
½ teaspoon each; chili powder, oregano and parsley flakes
1 tablespoon tamari

Sauté onion, pepper, *Nereocystis*, and garlic. Add lima beans, corn and seasonings. Simmer 5 to 10 minutes. Serve hot.

Cock & Bull Stew

1 stewing chicken
1 tablespoon oil

2 to 3 tomatoes
4 cloves garlic
1 cup water
2 teaspoons mineral seasoning (salt, veg. protein, horseradish,
    basil oregano, lemon, etc.) or your favorite mixture
1½ cups *Nereocystis* rings
2 cups carrot slices
2 cups potatoes, cut in chunks
3 tablespoons tamari (soy sauce)

Heat oil in heavy skillet. Brown chicken on all sides (cut up if desired). Add garlic and sauté lightly. Add tomatoes and water. Cover tightly and simmer 2 to 3 hours until tender. When almost done add carrots, potatoes, *Nereocystis* and soy sauce, and cook until vegetables are done. Bean sprouts or cut up green beans may also be added.

French Dressing

Vitamins and minerals leach away into the liquid residue during the pickling process. Instead of throwing it down the drain, why not use the liquid to make salad dressings!

½ teaspoon sugar or honey (opt.)
¼ teaspoon paprika
dash of pepper
½ teaspoon dry mustard
¼ cup *Nereocystis* dill pickle liquid

Place all ingredients in jar and shake. Add ½ cup oil gradually, shaking between additions. For variety, add garlic and 2 teaspoons Porphyra Salad (see recipe) seasonings. Chill and shake before pouring over salad greens.

Pizza de Ocean

Mussels combined with Nereocystis on Porphyra crust.

Crust:

2 cups sourdough starter	½ teaspoon salt
1 tablespoon active dry yeast	1 tablespoon oil
½ cup warm water	1 tablespoon honey
approx. 2 cups flour	⅓ cup *Porphyra* flour
	(see *Porphyra* section)

Mix together to very stiff bread dough consistency, adding more flour if needed. Let rise in warm place till double. Pat or roll thin, about ¼ inch, to fit oiled cookie sheets or pizza pans.

Sauce:

1 tablespoon oil
1 medium onion, diced
1 to 2 cloves grated garlic
2 cups shelled mussels (or 1 pound hamburger)
2 cans tomato sauce, 15 ounce
1 tablespoon Italian seasonings (oregano, marjoram, basil, etc.)
4 cups *Nereocystis*, thinly sliced, use bulb and stipe
¾ pound jack cheese, sliced

Place mussels in a covered pot and heat 15 minutes, or until shells open (no water necessary). Remove mussels from shell and measure about 2 cups.

Sauté onions and garlic in oil. Chop mussels if large, and add to onion and garlic, along with tomato sauce, *Nereocystis* and seasonings. Simmer 15 minutes or longer. Spread on *Porphyra* crust, top with cheese and bake at 400 degrees for 15 to 20 minutes, or until crust edges are brown. Serves 10.

If hamburger is used instead of mussels, brown meat with onions and garlic and simmer 15 minutes or longer with tomato sauce and seasonings before adding *Nereocystis*. Pizza may be garnished with sliced olives, pineapple, mushrooms, chopped green onions, or sliced tomatoes, etc., a few minutes before done.

Nereocystis Pizza with Tofu

Frozen tofu is especially nice in this recipe, because of its chewy, cheesiness.

1 sourdough pizza crust (or any pizza crust)
2 cups *Nereocystis* dill pickles, sliced and rinsed in water
1 pound frozen or fresh tofu
1 medium onion, diced
2 to 4 cloves garlic, minced or grated
¼ teaspoon cayenne
2 teaspoons Italian seasonings
6 ounces tomato paste

Sauté onions and garlic with tofu. Break up frozen tofu as it thaws. Add Italian seasoning and continue sautéing 15 to 20 minutes.

Roll out pizza crust and place on oiled pizza pan. Spread with tomato paste. Top with tofu mixture and *Nereocystis* dill pickle slices. Bake at 400 degrees, 15 minutes or until crust is brown. Bake in lower part of oven to assure crisp crust. Mozzarella or jack cheese may also be added to topping if desired.

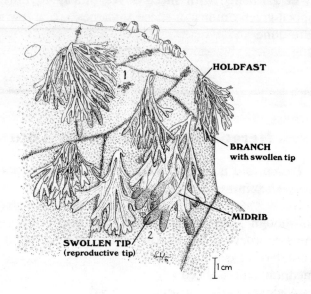

HOLDFAST

BRANCH
with swollen tip

MIDRIB

SWOLLEN TIP
(reproductive tip)

1 cm

1. Pelvetiopsis
2. Fucus

Pelvetiopsis limitata & Fucus

(pel vee tee op' sis; stir fry seaweed; fyoo' cus)

Description

    Color: Olive green to light tan

    Size: 3 to 7 inches (8 to 18cm) long

    Features: Small discoid holdfast, often encrusted with barnacles; repeatedly and equally branched. Branch tips of mature plants are swollen and covered with the fruiting structures. A miniature member of the *Fucus* group.

Habitat & Distribution

    Coastal areas: Alaska to California

    Tidal Condition: Upper to mid intertidal zone, occupying slightly higher rocks and ledges than its sea relative, *Fucus*, which occupies this same zone.

Foraging

Season: Late spring and summer

Instructions: For easy harvest, use scissors to avoid pulling loose the calcareous encrusted attachment with developing smaller plants. (Makes cooking preparations easier, too.)

Preparation

Preservation: Freeze – but as with other vegetables, it may be advisable to steam briefly before freezing to stop enzyme action and assure good quality for long storage. Dried *Pelvetiopsis* is quite inferior to fresh for stir fries, etc.

Note: *Pelvetiopsis,* found in the littoral zone, is littered with *Littorina*. Dip harvested *Pelvtiopsis* in fresh water to loosen and release clinging shells. Trim off holdfasts. Drain and store in refrigerator. It keeps well fresh for three to four weeks, or longer, making it one of the best sea vegetables for using fresh. Possibly keeps better if not rinsed in fresh water until used.

Use

Eaten raw, or cooked in soups and stir fries, *Pelvetiopsis* is one of our choicest seaweeds. It becomes tender very quickly, turning a bright green when heated.

Nutrients

Although no information is available, *Pelvetiopsis,* being related to *Fucus,* is probably relatively high in fats and oils (but not cholesterol), enabling it to withstand long periods of exposure. It should be high in iodine, vitamins, and other minerals and essential trace elements common to sea vegetables. *Pelvetiopsis* may be similar to *Fucus* in nutrition; high in magnesium, protein, vitamin A, iodine, bromine and phosphorus. *Fucus* contains the gels, fucoiden, alginic acid, and laminarin; it has also been reported to contain fats, vitamin C, calcium, sodium, sulfur, chloride, silicon, iron, manganese, copper, zinc, cobalt, titanium, hydrogen, molybdenum, lead, barium, boron, radium and trace elements. *Fucus* also contains iodamino acid, which has antilipemic and weight reducing properties. Fucoiden, the polysaccharide obtained from *Fucus* has a blood anticogulant effect equal to that of heparin. *Pelvetiopsis* and *Fucus* both become quite sticky with algin when mature.

Pelvetiopsis Stir fry

Many sea vegetables are delicious stir fried, including Alaria, Nereocystis, Macrocystis, Cystoseira, Postelsia, Analipus, Porphyra, Egregia bulbs, etc. But Pelvetiopsis is the preferred basis for a seaweed stir fry.

2 cups fresh or frozen *Pelvetiopsis*, thawed (other seaweeds may be used, cut or slice thinly)
3 tablespoons oil (some people prefer peanut oil, or sesame oil)
1 clove garlic, grated
small piece ginger, grated
½ cup sliced mushrooms
½ cup celery, chopped
¼ cup green pepper, chopped (opt.)
1 cup edible pod peas
1 medium onion chopped, or chopped green onions
3 to 4 tablespoons shoyu (soy sauce)
1 teaspoon Spike
½ cup sliced water chestnuts (opt.)
1 cup thinly sliced green beans, zucchini, or other vegetables in season (opt.)

Heat the oil in a skillet or wok. Start with the garlic and ginger: sauté and push to side. Add vegetables in turn, beginning with onions, mushrooms and sea vegetables and finishing with celery and water chestnuts, green onions and Spike. Cover and steam briefly to allow flavors to blend. A small amount of chicken or other stock may be used. For sweet and sour effect add about 1 teaspoon honey and 2 teaspoons vinegar. Serve with rice or noodles.

Sukiyaki or Chop Suey

1 recipe *Pelvetiopsis* stir fry, above
½ to 1 cup thinly sliced pork, chicken or beef, or tofu

Marinade the meat a few minutes if desired in sauce of 1 teaspoon each, cornstarch, sherry and shoyu. Start with the meat or tofu in wok with oil, garlic and ginger. When done, push to side and sauté vegetables as for stir fry above. Serve with noodles or rice.

Sweet and Sour Pelvetiopsis

3 tablespoons oil
4 tablespoons sunflower seeds
2 cups fresh *Pelvetiopsis*, washed and trimmed (frozen OK)
2 cups fresh tart apples, peeled and sliced
2 tablespoons honey
¼ cup raisins
1 teaspoon cinnamon

In skillet sauté sunflower seeds till slightly browned. Add *Pelvetiopsis* and sauté until tender. Add apple slices, raisins, cinnamon and honey. Continue to slowly cook a few minutes to blend flavors.

Fish & Rice Seaweed Dish

Makes four portions.

3 tablespoons oil
1 to 1½ pounds fish fillet such as red snapper
flour and salt
2 cups fresh or frozen seaweed or reconstituted dried seaweed,
  sliced or chopped. Use *Pelvetiopsis, Alaria, Postelsia* or
  Nereocystis
2 cups cooked brown or white rice
3 tablespoons soy sauce
1 tablespoon Spike, or other seasonings, to taste
1 tablespoon grated garlic

Sprinkle fish with small amount of flour and season sparingly with salt and pepper. In skillet sauté lightly in oil. Add garlic and seaweed and cook a few minutes. Add rice and remaining ingredients. Cover and cook gently over low heat about 20 minutes.

Pelvetiopsis (stir fry seaweed)

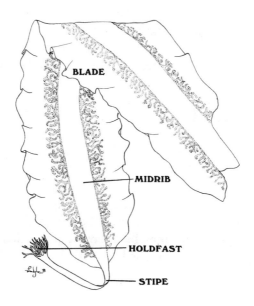

Pleurophycus gardneri

(plu ro fi' cus; sea spatula)

Description

Color: Golden brown, or light olive brown to very dark

Size: Single flat blade measures up to 3 feet (90cm) long and 16 inches (40cm) wide, midrib 2 to 6 inches (5 to 15cm) wide, stout stipe up to 20 inches (50cm) long

Features: Delicate taste; wide flat midrib that extends the length of the blade, delicately wavy and ruffled blade. Cylindrical at the base and more flattened near the blade, where it merges into the midrib.

Habitat & Distribution

Coastal Area: Alaska to Oregon

Tidal Condition: Lower intertidal and upper subtidal zones, found on rocks.

Foraging
Season: Late spring to autumn
Instructions: Attached plants may be gathered at low tides. Cast up plants often are found in good condition as well.

Preparation
Preservation: Dried.
Note: Fronds may be used fresh, or sundried and then hydrated before use. Stipes are used fresh.

Uses
Fresh or hydrated blades may be used in recipes for roll-ups similar to *Alaria*. Also may be steamed and used hot or chilled. Fresh stipes may be chopped and added to salads and stuffings. Also may be used to wrap fish for baking in coals.

Nutrition
Not much information on specific minerals and vitamins, or calories, but presumably very high in the vitamins and minerals common to brown sea vegetables, plus polysaccharides and gels similar to other kelps.

Recipes follow.

Tempeh Roll-ups

2 to 3 fronds *Pleurophycus* or *Alaria*
¾ pound tempeh
1 large clove garlic, grated

Tomato sauce topping:
8 ounce tomato sauce seasoned with 2 teaspoons Italian
   seasoning or 1 teaspoon Spike

Shoyu-wine topping:
4 to 5 tablespoons shoyu (tamari)
⅓ cup sherry
1 teaspoon Spike

Steam fresh seaweed over boiling water briefly to soften.
If using dried seaweed, reconstitute in water by soaking 15
minutes. Cut into 4 inch sections. Cut tempeh into 1 or 2 inch
pieces and wrap with seaweed. Place in small baking pan and
pour either of the above toppings on top. Cover with lid or foil
and bake about 30 minutes at 350 degrees.

Pleurophycus Stuffed with Pork or Tofu

Pleurophycus blades (fresh or dried)
1¼ pounds ground lean pork or tofu
1 cup chopped onions and garlic
1 cup brown rice
2 cups water
1 cup chopped fresh mushrooms
¼ cup chopped fresh parsley, or 2 tablespoons dried
½ pound cheddar cheese
3 tablespoons chopped almonds or walnuts
½ teaspoon mace
1 teaspoon grated fresh ginger

⅓ cup soy sauce (tamari)
2 teaspoons horseradish
⅛ teaspoon cayenne
toothpicks

Bring water to boil; add rice, cover, and simmer till done. Rinse the fresh *Pleurophycus*, or reconstitute dried kelp by soaking in cold water 30 minutes. Cut kelp into about 5 inch lengths.

In large skillet sauté pork. Add onions and garlic, or if using tofu heat oil, sauté onions and garlic and add tofu. Add cooked rice and other ingredients. Continue to sauté about 10 minutes, until ingredients are blended. Cool slightly and form into patties, using about 3 tablespoons for each patty. Lay one patty on end of each cut piece of kelp, and roll up, pinning it tightly with two toothpicks. Stack rolls in a steaming device and steam for about 45 minutes. Serve hot.

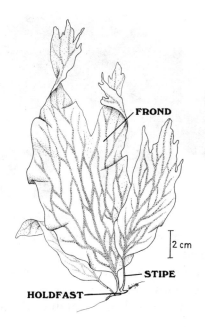

FROND

2 cm

STIPE

HOLDFAST

Polyneura latissima
(polly noo' rah)

Description
Color: Bright rose-red
Size: 4 to 10 inches (10 to 25cm) long, 4 to 6 inches (10 to 15cm) wide
Features: Occur in clusters. Blade is divided or lobed, and frays with age; is thin, fragile, has crinkly texture, conspicuous crisscrossed network of veins, small cylindrical stipe, and small discoid holdfast. Has iodine odor.

Habitat & Distribution
Coastal Area: Alaska to Mexico
Tidal Condition: Lowest part of the intertidal and subtidal zones to depths of 45 to 60 feet. Found on shaded sides of vertical surfaces of rocks, pilings, etc., near the low tide mark.

Foraging

Polyneura latissima

Season: Prime in early summer, dies back with intense light and heat.

Instructions: *Polyneura* grows most abundantly on shady sides of pilings or floating docks, where it may be easily plucked off, or reached by grappling if under water.

Preparation

Preservation: Dry thoroughly in sun and breeze to prevent mold, and then store in tight plastic bags or jars. May be frozen.

Note: Trim off holdfast and any calcareous patches of encrusting Bryozoa colonies. Wash quickly in tepid water to remove sand.

Uses

The Philippine community in San Francisco uses fresh, raw, blanched, dried, or frozen *Polyneura*. If dried, requires only brief soaking in water to reconstitute. To retain the lovely rose color, do not blanch. May be chopped or sliced, then added to soups, or as a garnish for salads. Particularily tasty with cottage cheese or tomato and onion salad (try vinegar and honey dressing).

Nutrients

Very high iodine. Additional information not available.

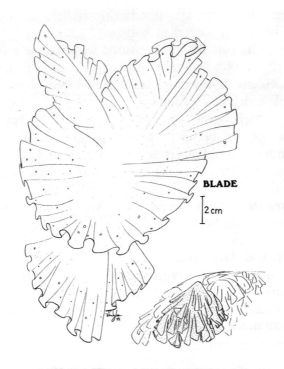

BLADE

2 cm

Porphyra species
(por fi' rah; nori or laver)

Description

Color: Several varities found on the west coast include: *Porphyra abbotta* - deep rose pink, red-brown with age; *P. nereocystis* - dull rose to purple red; and the most common *P. perforata* - green, steel gray, brownish purple, or black. On the east coast are: *P. leucosticta* - purplish, reddish or brown; *P. miniata* - rosy; and *P. umbilicalis* - purplish, reddish or brown.

Size: *Porphyra abbottae* - irregular shape up to 12 by 20 inches (30 to 50cm); *P. nereocystis* - up to 20 inches (50cm) wide by 4 feet (1.2m) long; *P. perforata* - up to 3 feet (.9m) long and 6 to 12 inches (15 to 30cm) wide. *P. leucosticta* - 6 inches (15cm) wide; *P. miniata* - 1 or more feet (30cm) long; *P. umibilicalis* - up to a foot (30cm) wide.

Features: *Porphyra* is very thin and elastic, resembling a piece of tightly stretched balloon. Satiny sheen and iridescence in the sun. May be confused with *Iridaea*, but *Porphyra* has a thinner blade, a texture stronger than *Iridaea*, and is not as iridescent. *P. perforata* are deeply lobed plants, thin and ruffled, with a discoid holdfast. *P. nereocystis* has large ruffled blade which grows epipytically on the stipes of older *Nereocystis* (bullwhip kelp). Begins growth in winter and continues throughout the next year into late autumn. *P. abbottae* has large, broad ruffled blades. *P. umbilicalis* is soft, paper-thin, nearly transparent, with ruffled blades. *P. leucosticta* features are same as *P. umbilicalis*. And *P. miniata* is similar to the preceeding two, but the blade is thicker.

Habitat & Distribution

Coastal Areas: West Coast species include *Porphyra perforata*, *P. abbottae* (Alaska, Washington, and British Columbia), *P. nereocystis*. There are several other species, about 20 in total. East Coast species are *Porphyra umbilicalis*, *P. leucosticta*, *P. miniata*.

Porphyra nereocystis (nori or laver)

Tidal Conditions: *P. abbottae* – mid intertidal regions; *P. lanceolata* – sometimes found in more sandy areas; *P. perforata* – mid to high intertidal regions. *P. leucosticta* – intertidal region; *P. miniata* – intertidal regions; *P. nereocystis* – subtidal, on stipes of *Nereocystis*; and *P. umbilicalis* – intertidal region.

Other species of *Porphyra* are occasionally found cast up from the lower depths, or growing attached to other plants, such as the *P. nereocystis* which grows on the stipes of *Nereocystis*.

Foraging

Season: Late spring is peak harvest, though *Porphyra* may be harvested into the summer and sometimes in autumn, but the quality decreases significantly.

Instructions: Pluck plants from the rocks. At peak harvest, fronds are small, later in the season the plants are larger and often have discolored patches. *P. perforata*, though large and abundant in late autumn, tends to be tough and less tasty than earlier in the season.

Preparation

Preservation: Sundried and stored in tight plastic bags or jars. May also be frozen.

Note: *Porphyra* should be washed quickly in several changes of water to remove sand and clinging shells. Drain thoroughly. Excess water may also be removed by centrifuging, as you would lettuce. It will keep several days if refrigerated.

Uses

Porphyra is one of our most delicious and versatile sea vegetables. *P. perforata*, used fresh, requires long cooking or tenderizing with soy sauce. When dry it may be toasted for a snack, or ground or flaked for bread, pastries, soups, etc.

Nutrients

Porphyra is very high in protein, contains carbohydrates

and almost no fat. It contains vitamins A, B₂ (riboflavin), niacin, B₁₂, plus C and D. It contains calcium, iron, iodine, phosphorus and trace elements. The delicious taste comes from astonishingly large numbers of compounds including nucleic acids and several amino acids; glutamic acid (base of MSG), alanine, which produces the sweet taste, glycine and taurine. Lowers blood cholesterol levels. *P. nereocystis* contains 50% more vitamin C than oranges and considerable quantities of B vitamins.

Table 9

Nutrient Content Of Nori
In Japan / 100 Gram Nori Sheets

Water	11.4g	Provitamin A	44,500. IU
Protein	35.6g	Vitamin B₁	.25 mg
Fat	.7g	Vitamin B₂	1.24 mg
Carbohydrate	44.3g	Niacin	10.00 mg
Ash	8.0g	Vitamin C	20. mg

More About Porphyra

From the culinary standpoint the various species of *Porphyra* represent the most important algal resource. About eighty species of this group of seaweeds are found in cool current tidal areas around the world. One of the tastiest, most versatile and easiest to harvest sea vegetable, the extraordinarily nutritious *Porphyra* contains many important vitamins and minerals, and provides a protein content of 30% or more (dry weight), comparable to other complete high protein foods. Made from several species of *Porphyra*, Japan's most important marine resource, "nori," is marketed in sheets measuring 19 by 20 cm. and weighing about 3 grams. A large part of Japan's production is exported to U.S. health food and ethnic food stores where it may cost up to $40 a pound or more.

Dried nori sheets contain 36,000 to 540,000 international units of vitamin A per 100 grams. Thus, one nori sheet provides vitamin A equivalent to a quarter pound of butter or 3 eggs, plus large amounts of vitamins B, C and D, and substances effective in reducing blood cholesterol.

Used in certain parts of Great Britain, sometimes as fresh salad, but more often cooked and made into breakfast cereal, is the thin, delicate *Prophyra laciniata*. Whaling crews in the 18th century used it to prevent scurvy, and large quantities are still used by miners of South Wales. In 1954, 213 tons were sold there. Today over 200 tons are harvested and processed annually in the British Isles. A popular recipe for its use is to thoroughly wash in fresh water and steep in pure water for 3 to 4 hours. Then boil gently until tender and pour off the water. Beat in a small amount of salt, then mix with oatmeal and fry as flatcakes. The cooked laver, mixed with vinegar or lemon juice, a few drops of olive oil, pepper and salt, reportedly is delicious served cold on toast; and equally as tasty with butter, gravy, lemon juice and pepper heated and served with roast meat.

In New Zealand, *Porphyra calumbero*, known as "karegna," and relished by the Maoris people, is used as a delicacy on special occasions and is prepared by steaming. In the Second World War, Maoris serving in the Middle East would chew *Porphyra* to relieve their thirst on desert marches.

Porphyra species occur in greater number and variety than any other seaweed on the Pacific Northwest Coast, attached to rocks in the mid to high intertidal. Native

Americans gathered large amounts of *Porphyra* and preserved it in several forms. One method, a complicated and somewhat unappetizing process, involved packing the *Porphyra* in boxes, interlayering it with cedar boughs and annointing it with chewed chiton to ferment and tenderize it. (Fortunately we now have soy sauce.) It was then torn in strips and chopped with adzes, chewed, and then boiled in a pot for long periods until tender. Some tribes made pressed, dried cakes or plugs of *Porphyra* which were shaved into warm water and boiled into a thick porridge. The simplest method, and one still used today, was to spread it out on rocks in the sun; when dry it was broken into small pieces and stored in large buckets or cans (or plastic bags). It was eaten dried, as a confection, or boiled with eulachon or candlefish grease, halibut heads, clams or creamed corn. A powder form was also made, similar to our recipes, by toasting freshly collected plants over the fire until lightly browned, and then beaten until frothy and served with fresh berries. This famous sea plant continues to serve as a food item, bartered between coastal and inland peoples.

Porphyra nereocystis, a West Coast species, only grows on the bullwhip kelp, *Nereocystis.* It is a very large, deep pink to dull red oval-shaped plant, and is found on the older *Nereocystis* stipes, and is quite beautiful when collected in autumn or early spring.

Several species of *Porphyra* are being investigated for culture. One of these, *P. abbottae* (named after the phycologist, Isabella Abbott) is considered especially tender and tasty. *P. torta* and *P. perforata,* also found in some quantity around the Puget Sound area, are being investigated for lab culture in Washington. *P. torta,* collected by Japanese researchers and grown in culture commercially for a brief time, occurs during the winter in the high intertidal zone.

Recipes follow.

Porphyra Flour

Very high in protein. For use in cakes, cookies, breads and toppings.

Wash freshly collected Porphyra in fresh water to remove sand and clinging shells. Do not soak. Shake and drain to remove as much water as possible. Spread it out to dry on screens in sun and breeze. May then be stored for a year or longer in tight plastic bags, or jars.

To make flakes or flour, place in pans in slow oven (around 300 degrees) for a few minutes until it turns green and becomes crisp enough to crush or grind into flour or flakes. A food blender works fine. It may be used as part of the flour in biscuits, pancakes, pie shells, cookies, etc. Substitute about ¼ to ½ cup *Porphyra* for the flour in a recipe. One cup dry *Porphyra* yields about 2 tablespoons flour. Flour can also be made from Healthful Porphyra Chips recipe.

Porphyra Pie Crust

Delicious for meat, cheese or vegetable pies.

1¾ cup wheat flour
¼ cup *Porphyra* flour
1 teaspoon salt
½ cup oil
3 to 4 tablespoons yogurt

Stir together the ingredients and roll out between two layers of waxed paper or plastic. Remove top layer of paper, invert over pie tin and pat to fit. Remove the piece of plastic or paper and flute edges of crust if desired. More *Porphyra* may be used, but rolling becomes difficult.

Super Biscuits

Very nutritious, if a little heavy.

2 cups biscuit mix
1 cup rolled oats
¼ cup *Porphyra* flour
¼ cup sesame seeds
⅔ cup dry skim milk or powdered milk
approx. ⅞ cup water

Mix dry ingredients. Add water to make dough. Roll out and cut, or drop. Bake on cookie sheet 10 to 12 minutes at 375 to 400 degrees.

Healthful Porphyra Chips

Like potato chips, only much better for you!

Snip dried *Porphyra* into 2 to 3 inch strips and bake at 250 degrees for 15 to 20 minutes until crisp. Caution – keep temperature low, and watch closely, as *Porphyra* burns easily. It will turn bright green. Prepare just before serving as they quickly become limp with absorbed moisture.

Or, rub dried *Porphyra* with oil by working teaspoons of oil over leaves with hands. Place in covered skillet, and heat until crisp, stirring frequently.

Porphyra Condiment or Topping

¼ cup peanut oil
1 cup dried *Porphyra*, whole or snipped into small pieces

Heat oil in skillet and fry the *Porphyra,* stirring until the pieces are crispy. Serve over eggs, meat, potatoes, fish, rice, etc.

Porphyra Bread

2 tablespoons honey
½ cup warm water
1 tablespoon yeast
2 cups sourdough starter
2 tablespoons margarine

½ teaspoon salt
2 eggs, beaten
3 cups wheat flour (approx.)
½ to 1 cup *Porphyra* flour

Dissolve yeast in warm water, add honey, sourdough starter, margarine, salt, eggs and flours, enough to make dough stiff enough to knead. Knead a few minutes, place in warm place to rise, punch down, shape into loaf or buns, and bake. Use 350 degree oven for buns, 15 minutes, and 325 degree oven for bread, 35 to 45 minutes.

Note: The amount of *Porphyra* may be increased, and the wheat flour decreased. *Porphyra* flour may also be added to any bread recipe for added nutrition.

Porphyra Sourdough
For Pizza or French Bread

½ cup warm water
1 tablespoon (one package) active dry yeast
2 cups thick sourdough starter
scant 2 cups flour (may use part or all whole wheat flour)
½ cup *Porphyra* flour (see recipe)
1 teaspoon honey
½ teaspoon salt

Dissolve yeast in warm water. Add honey and mix with

starter. Add remaining ingredients, using enough flour to make very stiff dough. Turn dough onto floured board and knead, using more flour if necessary. Knead 5 to 10 minutes for bread (for pizza less kneading is required).

Let rise in greased, covered bowl in warm place until doubled. Punch down, and shape into bread or buns, or roll very thin to fit pizza pans. Place dough into greased pans. When doubled, bake bread at 350 degrees, buns at 400 degrees. For crusty bread place pan of hot water in oven. For pizza, top with tomato topping made according to Pizza de Ocean recipe, or recipe for *Alaria* Lasagne or Pizza.

Tortillas

A substitute for tortillas may be made from the above recipe. Take bun-sized portions of raised dough, and roll very thin on board spread with fine cornmeal. Place on greased baking sheets, let rise a few minutes, and bake in very hot oven (400 to 450 degrees) a few minutes.

Korean Style Toasted Porphyra

1 tablespoon oil (use dark sesame oil if you have it)
1 tablespoon shoyu (soy sauce)
⅛ teaspoon cayenne
2 cups dried *Porphyra*

Combine oil, shoyu and cayenne in small bowl. Push *Porphyra* pieces down into the mixture. Turn, spread pieces with fingers, until uniformly coated. Place on large baking sheet. Bake at 300 degrees about 5 minutes, or until pieces turn greenish. Watch closely so they don't burn. Serve immediately as snack or crumble over dishes such as rice or salads.

Note: This may also be made by crisping *Porphyra* oil seasoned pieces in skillet over medium heat. For variations try adding ½ teaspoon lemon juice or other seasonings such as mustard or Spike.

Nori Pops

Must be made in a hot air popcorn popper.

½ cup dried *Porphyra* snipped to popcorn sized pieces
½ cup popcorn
¼ cup melted butter
1 teaspoon Hot Seas seasoning (see recipe)
2 teaspoons soy sauce

Put the pieces of nori into the bottom of the popper *first.* Add the popcorn, and turn it on. The nori will come out all crisp and crunchy with the popped corn. Add the soy sauce to the melted butter and pour on popcorn. Sprinkle with Hot Seas and serve.

Hot Seas Seasoning

Adapted from traditional Japanese 7 spice seasoning recipes, which were developed 300 years ago to warm the devoted worshipers after they had been sitting half-naked under cold water falls at the temples in Kyoto! According to Sharon Rhoads, author of Cooking With Sea Vegetables, *they included hemp seeds, but these are hard to find. Use as you would cayenne or chili powder in soups, etc. Sprinkle a bit on popcorn – really peps it up! Also good in guacamole.*

2 teaspoons crushed *Porphyra* (see recipe for *Porphyra* flour)
1 teaspoon poppy seeds
1 tablespoon sesame seeds
2 teaspoons ground dried sweet tangerine or orange peel
½ teaspoon pepper, or 1 teaspoon pepper corns
1 teaspoon ground mustard
½ to 1 teaspoon cayenne
2 teaspoons powdered kelp

Grind or blend all together thoroughly. This is easily made in a blender, but may also be made with mortar and pestle. Put in a shaker and use for a hot seasoning.

Seas All Seasoning

Blend in blender a mixture of equal parts *Porphyra* flour (see instructions) and the following dried herbs: oregano, marjoram, basil, thyme, rosemary, parsley, tarragon; and half as much celery seed and dill (not dill seed). Monosodium glutamate (MSG) may also be added. Store in jar for use in dressings or as Italian seasoning. Kelp powder may also be added for boosted flavor and nutrition.

Yogurt and Mayonnaise Dressing

2 teaspoons Seas All Seasoning
2 cups yogurt
2 cups mayonnaise or salad dressing
1 to 2 cloves garlic, grated

Stir all together.

Russian Tofu Dressing

½ pound tofu
2 teaspoons Seas All Seasoning
2 tablespoons oil
2 tablespoons lemon juice
1 to 2 cloves garlic
¼ cup ketchup
1 teaspoon tamari
½ teaspoon curry (opt.)

Blend all ingredients in blender till smooth.

Italian Tofu Dressing

½ pound tofu
1 teaspoon Seas All Seasoning
4 tablespoons any oil and vinegar dressing (or 1½ tablespoons
    vinegar and 3 tablespoons olive oil)
1 to 2 cloves garlic, grated
1 tablespoon tahini

Mash or blend tofu and add remaining ingredients.
Note: Brine from any of *Nereocystis* Dills can be used in this recipe, and will provide minerals and vitamins leached out of the sea vegetable pickles.

Creamy Tofu Mayo

½ pound tofu
1 teaspoon Seas All Seasoning
1 tablespoon vinegar, or use 2 tablespoons of brine from
    Nereocystis Dill Pickles

1 teaspoon miso
2 teaspoons prepared mustard
½ teaspoon honey
2 tablespoons oil

Blend all but oil in blender until smooth. Continue blending and slowly add oil.

Porphyra Corn Fritters

Delicious! Serves three.

3 tablespoons *Porphyra* flour
2 to 3 ears of corn, scraped from cob (about 1 to 1 ½ cups)
2 egg yolks
½ cup sourdough starter
2 tablespoons dry skim milk powder
1 tablespoon oil
½ teaspoon salt
2 egg whites, beaten stiff

Combine *Porphyra*, corn, egg yolks, sourdough, milk powder, oil and salt. Fold in beaten egg whites. Sauté as for pancakes until brown – don't overcook. Serve plain, or with preferred toppings, such as butter, syrup, honey, jam and yogurt.

Seaweed Quiche

1 *Porphyra* pie crust (see recipe)
3 eggs, beaten
1 cup cream
½ cup milk

1 medium onion, diced
2 tablespoons oil
1 cup sliced mushrooms
½ cup sliced *Alaria* (if dried, soak in cold water)
1 teaspoon prepared mustard
¼ teaspoon cayenne
1 cup shredded Swiss cheese

Sauté onions, mushrooms and *Alaria* until liquid is evaporated and place in shell. Combine eggs, milk, etc. Pour over mushroom and Alaria mixture and bake about 45 minutes in 350 degree oven, or until set. Place in lower part of oven to assure well done crust.

Eggs in Nests

Porphyra (use fresh or dried)
eggs
oil
tamari or soy sauce
seasonings as desired (blend of oregano, marjoram, rosemary, parsley, tarragon)

Use ⅓ cup fresh *Porphyra*, or 2 tablespoons dry *Porphyra* for each serving, plus eggs and oil. Rinse fresh *Porphyra*, do not soak or dampen dry porphyra. Chop or shred coarsely, and sauté in skillet in oil and soy sauce till tender or crisp as desired, over medium heat. It will turn green.

Make a nest for each egg by pushing the cooked seaweed into circles. Crack one egg into each circle. Continue cooking till eggs are done.

Egg Foo Young with Porphyra

½ pound raw prawns – shelled, deveined, cut into pea sized
bits
2 cups fresh bean sprouts (¼ pound) rinsed and drained
6 to 8 eggs, beaten with ½ teaspoon salt (opt.)
¼ cup *Porphyra* flour (see instructions)
¼ cup sunflower or sesame seeds
½ cup slivered onions
1 clove minced garlic (opt.)
1 teaspoon Spike seasoning
1 cup fresh mushrooms, cleaned and sliced
½ teaspoon ginger root, grated
2 tablespoons tamari (soy sauce)

In frying pan on high heat using oil to coat food, sauté
prawns or other meat with garlic and ginger until meat turns
gray to white; transfer to colander with a bowl beneath it to
catch juice. Sauté seeds and *Porphyra*. Sauté vegetables in turn,
with seasonings, using part of the sautéed seeds and *Porphyra*
with each batch. Transfer to colander with prawns.

Mix drained prawns, vegetables, etc. into beaten eggs.
Starting on high heat, spoon mixture about ½ inch thick into
frying pan with about 2 tablespoons oil. Cook until golden
brown. Turn to brown other side, adding more oil if needed.
Pile the cooked cakes on a platter and serve with Egg Foo
Young Sauce.

Egg Foo Young Sauce:
1½ tablespoons cornstarch
2 tablespoons soy sauce
1 tablespoon plum sauce or apricot sauce
1 cup chicken broth plus 1 teaspoon chicken flavored soup
base

Put ingredients in sauce pan, stir over heat until boiling.
Use as topping for Egg Foo Young.

Quick Egg Foo Young

1¼ tablespoons oil
1 blade of dried *Porphyra* torn in pieces, or 1 sheet nori
2 tablespoons sunflower seeds or sesame seeds
2 to 3 mushrooms
¼ cup chopped onion
dash of fresh grated garlic and ginger if available
herbs as desired, such as dash of Spike
1 cup bean sprouts or mix of other vegetables, such as sliced
    celery, carrots, summer squash, or edible pod peas.
1 tablespoon tamari (soy sauce)
2 to 3 eggs

Heat oil in skillet. Lightly fry *Porphyra* and seeds until
Porphyra is green and crisp, and seeds are brown. Remove from
skillet. Sauté onions, mushrooms, sprouts, tamari, and
seasonings, lightly. Add beaten eggs and cook until partially
set, lowering heat. Turn with spatula, and cook until done.
Serve topped with crisp seeds and *Porphyra*.
Note: This is delicious served for breakfast. Small pieces
of ham cooked with the vegetables may be added.

Fresh Porphyra Soup

1 to 2 cups fresh *Porphyra* firmly packed
2 tablespoons shoyu (soy sauce)
½ cup chopped onion
1 fresh garlic or leek
8 cups water
¼ cup brown rice
¼ cup split peas
1 carrot, diced
1 tomato, diced (opt.)
2 teaspoons Italian seasonings

Wash *Porphyra* in several changes of water, lifting out to remove sand and shells which settle to the bottom. Drain and place in pot with oil. Heat and stir until *Porphyra* is wilted and green. Add shoyu, chopped onion and garlic and continue cooking 5 to 10 minutes, stirring occasionally. Add remaining ingredients, bring to boil and reduce heat. Simmer about 2 hours until tender. Season to taste with salt and pepper.

Temple Minestrone

This recipe's secret is Hot Seas Seasoning.

1 cup garbanzos (or kidney beans) soaked overnight in water to
    cover or one #300 can beans
1 cup dried *Porphyra*
2 tablespoons oil
1 clove garlic, diced
1 onion, sliced
2 cups water
2 cups canned tomatoes and juice
1 teaspoon Italian seasonings or *Porphyra* salad seasonings
3 teaspoons Hot Seas Seasoning
1 teaspoon basil
½ cup diced celery
2 cups diced zucchini
1 small carrot, diced

Place *Porphyra* and oil in skillet over moderate heat. Turn pieces until they are green and crisp. Break with fork into small pieces. Add onion and garlic, and sauté a few minutes. Add tomatoes, garbanzos or kidney beans, water and seasonings. Cook until beans are almost tender (about 2 hours). Add remaining vegetables and simmer a few minutes longer, until tender. Top with grated parmesan cheese and serve with garlic buttered French bread, if desired.

Mulligatawny Soup

A curried soup of East Indian origin. Alaria, or other seaweeds may also be used.

1 cup *Porphyra*, dried and crisped in oven and crumbled
½ pound tofu, frozen and thawed and cut into cubes
½ cup oil
½ cup onions, chopped
1 carrot, sliced
1½ cups chopped celery (or use part *Alaria*, soaked and sliced)
1½ tablespoons flour
2 teaspoons curry powder
2 teaspoons Spike (opt.)
2 cups water plus vegetable bouillon, or use stock
1 cup stewed or canned tomatoes, chopped
⅓ cup chopped apple
½ cup milk, or soy milk
salt, pepper, or soy sauce to taste

Freeze and thaw tofu, squeeze dry, cut into ½ inch cubes. Sauté vegetables and seaweed in oil in large pot. Stir in flour and curry; simmer 3 minutes. Crisp *Porphyra*, crumble and add with water, tofu cubes, tomatoes and apples. Simmer 15 minutes. Add salt, pepper, and if desired, soy sauce, to taste. Stir in milk, heat and serve immediately. Top with dab of sour cream if desired.

Sea Vegetable Minestrone For A Crowd

Made with dried Porphyra and Alaria, two delicious sea vegetables. Nori may substitute the Porphyra, and cabbage and spinach the Alaria. Fast and delicious. Serves twenty.

1 cup dried *Porphyra*

1 cup dried *Alaria* or 3 cups shredded cabbage and ½ pound
    spinach
¾ cups dry kidney beans
3 cups water for soaking beans
1¼ gallons beef stock or water plus 12 cubes bouillon or vege-
    X cubes, or use tamari to substitute part or all
1 bay leaf
½ teaspoon salt (more if needed)
2 teaspoons chili powder or ½ teaspoon cayenne (opt.)
½ teaspoon pepper
3 cloves garlic, minced
2 teaspoons Spike (opt.)
2 cups chopped onions
1½ cups chopped carrots
1½ cups chopped celery
1½ cups chopped potatoes
1½ cups chopped green beans
¼ cup parsley flakes or ½ cup fresh parsley
40 ounces tomato sauce
½ to 1 cup small elbow macaroni
other vegetables may be added - zucchini peeled and chopped,
    etc.

Soak kidney beans overnight. Add *Porphyra* which has
been finely cut with scissors.*Bring beans and seaweed to boil
and cook gently until beans are almost tender (about 1½
hours). Measure water or stock into large pot. Add beans and
remaining ingedients. Bring to boil, reduce heat and simmer
about 2 hours. If desired thicken with ½ cup flour blended in
¾ cup cold water.

Serve with grated cheese or Parmesan cheese, if desired. In
1981 this recipe cost only 15 cents a serving without cheese,
and with the garlic, green beans and seaweed donated.

***Note:** To quickly tenderize *Porphyra*, sauté briefly in
hot oil in wok or small skillet. Don't allow it to burn. It will
become greenish and crisp. Remove from heat and crush. May
also be crisped in moderate oven.

Tempeh Jambolaya

Sea-Soy Soup

½ cup *Porphyra* (nori) snipped into pieces
1 package tempeh (12 ounces) cut into cubes
1¼ cups chopped onions
2 cloves garlic, diced or grated
1 cup chopped celery
1 to 3 tablespoons oil
1 can tomatoes, 28 ounce
1 can tomato sauce, 8 ounce
1½ quarts water
1 to 2 teaspoons each: chili powder, cumin, coriander and salt
¼ to ½ cups brown rice cooked in 1 cup water
1 green pepper, diced (opt.)
pepper and Spike (opt.) to taste

Brown tempeh in heated oil in skillet or wok. Continue to brown and add snipped *Porphyra*. Cook slowly until *Porphyra* is crisp. Break up any large pieces of *Porphyra*. Add chopped onion and garlic and cook until soft. Add tomatoes, celery, seasonings, rice and water. Simmer 1 hour or longer to allow seasonings to blend, and the tempeh to absorb the flavor.

Native American Bean Soup

1 cup black beans (sometimes called turtle beans)
3 cups water (plus 4 to 5 cups later)
½ orange with peel
1 teaspoon each, coriander, cumin, chili powder and basil
½ teaspoon celery seed
½ sweet potato, peeled and grated
½ cup dried *Porphyra*
2 tablespoons oil

1 onion, chopped
2 cloves garlic, minced
1½ cups cooked rice
3 cups canned (or fresh) tomatoes
2 tablespoons tamari (soy sauce)
1 tablespoon *Nereocystis* dill pickle liquid or 1 teaspoon
   vinegar
½ cup each: chopped green pepper and celery (opt.)

Bring beans to boil in 3 cups water. Turn off heat, let
stand 1 to 2 hours. Drain. Sauté *Porphyra* in oil over medium
heat until greenish (watch so it doesn't burn). Add chopped
onions and garlic and sauté a few minutes. Combine with
beans plus 3 cups water and seasonings. Bring to boil, simmer
2 to 3 hours. Add remaining ingredients, and continue
simmering ½ hour. Add more liquid, if desired for soup; or
allow liquid to evaporate for a baked-bean dish.

Black On Black Bean Soup

*Named so because of the color similarity of the dark beans
and nori.*

1 cup dried or fresh *Porphyra*, snipped into small pieces
1½ cups black beans (turtle beans)
1½ quarts water
2 tablespoons oil
2 cloves elephant garlic, grated or chopped
1 onion, chopped
1 carrot, chopped
1 stalk celery with leaves and 1 medium potato chopped (opt.)
1 teaspoon Spike or mixture of oregano, savory, thyme,
   marjoram, basil and rosemary
¼ teaspoon pepper
⅛ teaspoon cayenne

1 teaspoon oregano
¼ teaspoon basil or savory
1 teaspoon cumin
16 ounces tomato sauce
salt to taste
sour cream (opt.)

Wash beans and soak overnight or use the quick soaking method. (Bring beans to a boil, reduce heat and simmer for 5 minutes. Remove from heat and let stand 2 hours before continuing cooking.) Black beans may also be cooked without soaking first, but it takes longer.

Soak dried *Porphyra* a few minutes in cold water (see note). Sauté onions and garlic in oil. Add with remaining vegetables, seasonings and tomato sauce to beans and *Porphyra*. Bring to boil and lower heat. Simmer slowly 3 to 4 hours. Adjust seasonings, add more if desired. Each bowl of soup may be topped with a dab of sour cream.

Note: To quickly tenderize *Porphyra*, sauté dried seaweed in hot oil in wok or small skillet. It will become greenish and crisp. Don't allow it to burn., Remove from heat and crush.

Lentil Soup With Porphyra

A hearty, full-bodied soup, high in protein.

1 cup dried *Porphyra*
2 tablespoons oil
5 cups water (plus vegetable bouillon, opt.) or stock
1 cup lentils, washed and drained
1 medium onion, diced
1 medium carrot, diced
½ cup diced celery
½ pound tofu, cut in small cubes (opt.)

2 or 3 cloves elephant garlic, grated
1 teaspoon Spike (opt.)
1 to 2 teaspoons each of cumin, coriander and chili powder
½ teaspoon each oregano, basil and marjoram
1 tablespoon shoyu (opt.)
1 eight ounce can tomato sauce, or chopped tomatoes
salt, pepper to taste

Bring lentils to boil in large pot. Crisp nori in moderate oven and crush (or in skillet sauté in oil until crisp and green; remove and crush).

Sauté onions and garlic, and add with other ingredients except tofu and tomatoes to boiling lentils. Simmer 1 hour.

Add tofu and remaining ingredients and simmer another hour or until lentils are tender. May be flavored with 1½ teaspoons wine vinegar.

Fish & Rice with Nori

2 cups rice
3 cup water
6 tablespoons sake or sherry
4 tablespoons tamari
salt to taste

1 tablespoon honey
½ pound loose-fleshed fish (bass, turbot, etc.)
¼ cup dried *Porphyra*, snipped in small pieces

Boil rice with 2 tablespoons tamari, 3 cups water, and ¼ cup sake or sherry for 30 to 45 minutes. Spoon onto serving dish, keep warm.

Cook fish in lightly salted water, drain, remove skin and bones, wrap in cloth and rub the flesh lightly until it flakes. Place fish in heavy skillet with honey, 2 tablespoons sake, 2 tablespoons tamari. Cook, stirring briskly to prevent sticking, until the fish becomes dry in texture. Arrange fish over the rice. Crisp the *Porphyra* in a slow oven, as for chips in recipe above, and crumble over the fish and rice as a garnish.

Porphyra Corn Pudding

Similar to recipe that was popular with Indians and colonial population in British Columbia.

½ cup dried *Porphyra* packed into measuring cup, crisped in oven and crumbled into small pieces
2 cups corn (cut from cob) or 2 cups canned cream style corn
1½ cups evaporated milk, or 1 cup milk and ½ cup cream
2 tablespoons pimentos or red sweet bell pepper, chopped
1 tablespoon margarine
1 tablespoon finely diced mild onion (opt.)

Combine ingredients in bowl and pour into margarine greased baking dish. Bake for 45 minutes at 350 degrees. Serve garnished with finely chopped onion (opt.).

Salal Berry Bars

Huckleberries or blueberries may also be used.

1 cup crushed *Porphyra*
¼ cup margarine melted
¼ cup brown sugar
1 teaspoon cinnamon
4 tablespoons bisquik mix
2 cups salal berries
1 egg
4 tablespoons bisquik

Prepare crushed *Porphyra* by toasting dried *Porphyra* in slow oven (250 to 300 degrees) a few minutes so that it turns green and crisp. Crush with fingers and measure. Mix *Porphyra* with melted margarine, sugar, cinnamon and 4 tablespoons bisquik.

Combine salal berries, egg and 4 tablespoons bisquik. Put half of *Porphyra* mixture on bottom of small pan. Cover with salal berry mixture and top with remaining *Porphyra* mixture. Bake at 350 degrees for 20 to 25 minutes.

Salal Berry Pie

1 recipe *Porphyra* pie crust, in deep 9 inch pie tin
3½ cups salal berries
1 cup rhubarb (1 additional cup salal berries plus 3 table-
    spoons lemon juice could be substituted)
1 cup sugar or ½ to ⅔ cup honey
½ cup sour cream
3 eggs, beaten
½ package lemon cake mix or crumb topping below

Mix sugars, beaten eggs, and sour cream, with 3 cups salal berries and rhubarb. Place in unbaked pie shell and top with dry cake mix or crumb topping. Sprinkle with ½ cup salal berries. Bake at 350 degrees for 45 minutes or until set.

Crumb topping:
Stir together until crumbly:
½ cup brown sugar
½ cup flour
¼ cup margarine
dash cinnamon

Oatmeal Cookies

1 cup margarine
1 cup white sugar
½ cup brown sugar (or use 1½ cups brown and no white)

1 beaten egg
1½ cups flour
1 teaspoon soda
1 teaspoon cinnamon
1 cup rolled oats
½ cup porphyra flour
¾ cup finely chopped nuts

Cream together margarine and sugars. Add egg and 1 teaspoon vanilla and mix well. Stir together flour, soda and cinnamon and add to mixture. Stir in oats, *Porphyra* flour and nuts.

Chill dough for 1 hour. Shape into walnut-sized balls and place on greased cookie sheet. Butter bottom of glass, dip in sugar and flatten the balls. Resugar glass each time. Bake at 350 degrees for ten minutes. Cool on rack. Makes about 4 dozen.

Banana Peanut Cookies

2 eggs, beaten
½ cup honey
1 large ripe banana, mashed (about ½ cup)
½ cup crunchy peanut butter
½ cup *Porphyra* flour (see recipe)
1½ cup whole wheat flour
½ teaspoon baking powder
1 teaspoon soda
½ teaspoon salt
1½ teaspoon cinnamon
½ teaspoon nutmeg
1 cup sunflower seeds
1 cup chocolate or carob chips (opt.)

Blend egg, honey, banana, peanut butter and *Porphyra* flour thoroughly. Stir together flour, spices, leavening, and

186 – Sea Vegetables

combine with egg mixture. Add sunflower seeds and chocolate chips. Drop by spoonfuls onto greased cookie sheet. Bake 10 to 12 minutes at 350 degrees.

Carrot Cake

⅓ cup *Porphyra* flakes (see recipe)
1¾ cups whole wheat flour
2 teaspoons baking powder
½ teaspoon soda
½ teaspoon salt
2 teaspoons cinnamon
2 teaspoons vanilla
1 cup honey
½ cup raisins (opt.)
½ cup nut meats or seeds (opt.)
2 eggs, beaten
½ cup margarine, melted
½ cup crushed pineapple with juice
2 cups grated carrots

Mix *Porphyra* with pineapple, set aside. In mixing bowl, combine whole wheat flour, baking powder, soda, salt and cinnamon. Mix in nuts or seeds and raisins. Mix beaten eggs with honey in small bowl. Combine egg mixture, pineapple mixture, melted margarine and carrots with flour mixture, and mix with a few strokes. Bake in a 8 or 9 inch greased pan, or ring mold, at 325 degrees about 50 minutes or until a fork or toothpick inserted into the cake comes out dry. Cream together icing below and spread on cooled cake.

Cream Cheese Icing:
4 ounces cream cheese
½ cup honey
½ teaspoon vanilla

Blackberry Jam Cake

1 cup margarine
2 cups sugar or 1½ cup honey
1 teaspoon baking soda
1 cup yogurt or buttermilk
4 large, or 5 medium eggs, separated
3 cups flour (whole wheat or white)
⅓ to ½ cup *Porphyra* flour (see recipe p. 165)
2 teaspoons cinnamon
1 teaspoon each of nutmeg, cloves, and allspice
1 teaspoon vanilla
1 cup blackberry jam

Cream together butter and honey. Dissolve soda in yogurt and add egg yolks. Mix flour and spices and *Porphyra* flour. Add with egg-yogurt mixture to creamed mixture alternately, blending after each addition. Add vanilla and jam and mix.

Beat egg whites until stiff. Fold into batter. Bake in large greased and floured tube pan at 300 degrees for 15 minutes, increase to 350 degrees and bake 45 minutes longer, or until done.

Brown Sugar Bars

¼ cup *Porphyra* flour   1 cup brown sugar
½ cup whole wheat flour   1 teaspoon vanilla
1 teaspoon baking powder   1 egg
¼ cup margarine   ¾ cup nuts or sunflower seeds
chocolate or carob chips (opt.)

Melt margarine in sauce pan. Stir in brown sugar, beat in egg. Mix together dry ingredients and stir in. Add vanilla. Spread in 9 by 11 inch baking pan, sprinkle with nuts or seeds and bake about 20 minutes at 350 degrees or until done. If desired, sprinkle chocolate chips or carob chips on top while hot.

Apple Dessert

Filling:
1 cup dried Alaria
2 cups apple slices (use tart apple)
½ cup yogurt
2 tablespoons honey

Crumb topping and crust:
1 cup *Porphyra*
¼ cup margarine
¼ cup brown sugar
¼ cup bisquik mix or flour

Prepare *Porphyra* flakes by heating the seaweed in oven till crisp, and then crumbling with fingers.

Mix together *Alaria* filling and allow to stand 15 minutes. Mix *Porphyra* topping and crust. Place half of *Porphyra* mixture in bottom of small baking pan. Place filling on crumb mixture and top with remaining *Porphyra* crumb mix. Bake at 325 to 350 degrees about 20 minutes.

French Pancakes

Serve with jelly or creamed Alaria inside.

10 tablespoons bread flour (scant ⅔ cup)
2 tablespoons *Porphyra* flour
½ teaspoon salt
1 teaspoon baking powder
2 tablespoons powdered sugar
2 eggs, beaten
⅔ cup milk
⅓ cup water
½ teaspoon vanilla, or ½ teaspoon grated lemon rind

Mix together dry ingredients. Beat eggs and add remaining liquid ingredients. Make a well in the dry ingredients. Pour in the liquid ingredients. Combine with a few swift strokes (lumps do not matter). Heat a 5 inch skillet. Oil with a few drops of oil. Add a small quantity of batter, tipping skillet to spread, and cook over moderate heat, turning each pancake when brown and cooking on other side. Use a few drops of oil for each pancake.

For jelly variation, spread with filling of jelly, roll up and sprinkle lightly with confectioner's sugar. Or fill with creamed *Alaria*, omitting jelly and sugar (see recipe for creamed *Alaria*).

Tempura

Many different sea or land vegetables may be cooked this way. Delicious with sauce.

Batter # 1
½ cup flour
½ cup cornstarch
1 teaspoon salt
½ teaspoon MSG
1½ teaspoon baking powder
1 egg
⅔ cup water

Batter # 2
1 cup flour
½ teaspoon sugar
1 tablespoon shoyu
1 egg
¾ cup milk

Batter # 3
⅔ cup whole wheat flour
2 tablespoons cornstarch
1½ tablespoons sesame seeds
2 eggs, beaten
2 tablespoons fresh parsley, chopped fine
¼ teaspoon cayenne

Batter # 4
From Olympic Sea Gardens.
pinch baking soda
5 tablespoons flour
1 egg white
½ cup water

Clean about 1 pound of fresh *Porphyra* or other vegetable and drain well. Cut into 2 inch pieces. Dried nori may be first marinaded in 1½ cups water, 2 tablespoons soy sauce, 1 tablespoon rice vinegar, and 1 teaspoon sugar, for 1 hour.

Sift together all dry ingredients of the batter you are using. Beat together all wet ingredients in a separate bowl. Pour wet into dry and stir quickly. The batter should be lumpy. Prepare the batter just before you use it.

Heat 1 to 2 inches of cooking oil in a deep fat fryer or heavy kettle to 350 degrees. Dip drained pieces of seaweed or vegetable into batter, let excess drip off, and gently drop into heated oil. The pieces should sink to bottom and immediately bob back to top. If they don't, oil is too cold. If they brown too quickly, the oil is too hot. Fry a few pieces at a time until golden. Remove with slotted spoon and drain on paper towels. Serve immediately, with dipping sauce below.

Tempura Dipping Sauce:
3 cups dashi or chicken stock (see *Laminaria* recipes for dashi)
2 tablespoons soy sauce
1 tablespoon sugar or ½ tablespoon honey
½ teaspoon MSG (opt.)

Combine and pour into individual dipping bowls. Have a small bowl of grated daikon (Japanese radish) to mix with the sauce.

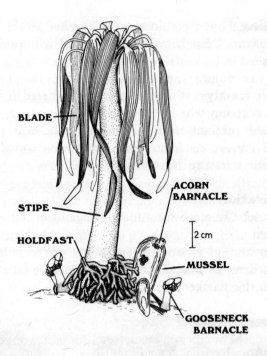

BLADE

ACORN
BARNACLE

STIPE

HOLDFAST

2 cm

MUSSEL

GOOSENECK
BARNACLE

Postelsia Palmaeformis
(pos tel' see ah; sea palm)

Description
Color: Rich olive brown
Size: Up to 2 feet (.6m) tall
Features: Resembles a midget palm tree, sturdy holdfast, hollow upright stipe bending to the surf, a crown of longitudinally grooved strap-shaped blades ½ to 1 inch wide. They often grow in clumps, when struck by waves the elastic stipe is bent almost horizontal, but regains its upright position as soon as the water recedes.

Habitat & Distribution
Coastal Areas: British Columbia to central California
Tidal Conditions: Strong surf, found on outer rocks and cliffs – often found in association with mussels and barnacles.

Foraging

Season: Peak harvest is in spring and summer; is an annual.

Instructions: Sometimes accessible, but often difficult to reach. Freshly cast up plants can be gathered. If fresh, stipes will snap crisply when bent. *Postelsia* doesn't regenerate easily, and faces extinction in California where it is gathered extensively. A considerate forager will leave enough plants on each site to assure reseeding.

Preparation

Preservation: Stipes may be pickled; blades may be sundried.

Note: The plants are usually free of unwanted material, and need no particular attention. They may be stored a few days in the refrigerator.

Postelsia (sea palm)

Uses

Postelsia has a superior flavor and texture. The stipes and blades may be used in many ways, similar to *Nereocystis*. They may be steamed or added to soups, stir fried, etc. Sundried blades can be eaten as snacks.

Recipes follow.

Sea Palm Zucchini-Cheese Omelet

2 tablespoons oil
2 cups zucchini slices or pieces
1 cup sliced sea palm stipe and fronds
1 garlic clove, grated
⅓ cup chopped onion
¼ cup sausage (opt.)
¼ cup sliced mushrooms (opt.)
4 eggs, beaten
½ to 1 cup other vegetable (opt.) such as sliced green beans, tomato, pod peas, broccoli, etc.
1 teaspoon Italian seasonings or Spike
salt and pepper to taste
½ cup jack cheese sliced in small pieces

Sauté sausage, if using. Add onion, garlic, sliced sea palm and zucchini, and other optional vegetables. Sprinkle with seasonings. Sauté gently a few minutes to evaporate some of the moisture. Pour beaten eggs on top. Top with cheese. Cover and cook slowly 10 to 15 minutes until eggs are set and the cheese is melted.

Sea Palm and Ogo Salad

Postelsia and Gracilaria sea vegetables are used here.

½ tomato chopped
¼ cup sliced onion or ½ cup chopped green onions
½ cup *Gracilaria* steamed briefly then chopped and chilled
¼ cup sliced *Postelsia* stipes and fronds, steamed
    and chilled
cottage cheese

Dressing:
2 tablespoons shoyu
2 tablespoons wine (sherry) opt.
1 teaspoon sugar or ½ tablespoon honey
1 teaspoon wine vinegar
½ teaspoon salt
¼ teaspoon pepper

Steam sea vegetables very briefly, chill and chop. Arrange mixed vegetables around cottage cheese, top with dressing.

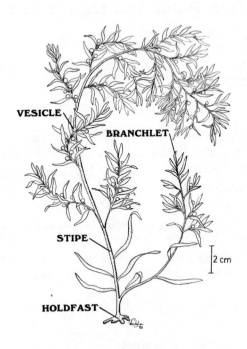

VESICLE

BRANCHLET

STIPE

2 cm

HOLDFAST

Sargassum
(sar gas' sum)

Description
Color: Yellowish brown

Size: Up to 6 feet (2m) long

Features: Resembles *Cystoseira*, but has smaller air bladders or floats which are usually borne singly and are more spherical in shape; small leaf-like blades have toothed, or serrated edges.

Habitat & Distribution
Coastal Area: California to Vancouver Island (came as a stowaway on oysters from Japan)

Tidal Condition: Often appears in bays and lagoons, and on rocks in low intertidal

Foraging

Season: Late spring to autumn
Instructions: Cut outer portions of plant
Preparation: Juvenile fronds are used fresh in soups, etc.; sundried for storage

Uses

Hawaiians used several species of *Sargassum* in their ceremonies, and also medicinally as a poultice for coral cuts. They used the leaves as stuffing for baked fish, or fresh with raw fish or octopus. Sundried leaves may be eaten like potato chips. The leaves may also be deep fried in a tempura batter, or added to seafood chowders and soups. Hawaiians also deep fat fry the leaves as a chip, or crushed and served on a fish casserole. The cleaned leaves are washed, patted dry, then fried at 375 degrees a few at a time, then drained and seasoned with salt.

Nutrition

Sargassum species contain fatty acids which are highly antibacterial. It also is being investigated for use as a blood anticoagulant, and for effects against tumors and sarcomas.

Other Sea Vegetables

It would take a much larger book to describe the hundreds of seaweeds encountered on forging trips. But I would be remiss not to just mention a few other abundant possible candidates for your table, many closely related to species used in other countries.

The green sea vegetable group have found favor in many cuisines, and being especially high in iron and protein, have much to offer to nutrition. In many harbors sea lettuce, *Ulva*, is the dominant alga, growing so luxuriantly in places that there's hardly room for other seaweeds. *U. lactuca* is one of the most widespread of *Ulva* in Northwest waters. Bright green in color, these thin sheets are often rather crinkly. The size and growth form is variable, depending on water conditions. Some *Ulva* species are very large, a yard or more in width. A common species in the Puget Sound region is *U. fenestrata*, which may or may not be perforated. Similar to it is *Ulvaria fusca*, (*Monostroma fuscum*), which begins growth as a bright green sac. This breaks open into a flat, single cell thick sheet which becomes olive in color as it ages. *Enteromorpha linza*, like *Ulva* is bright green, but grows in the shape of flattened tubes. Some specimens reach a length of 12 to 16 inches and may be twisted or ruffled. A smaller species, *E. intestinalis*, which occurs world-wide, is sold in many countries. (See Commercial Sea Vegetable Product section.) It tolerates a wide range of water conditions, including low salinity. *Codium fragile*, a blackish-green alga abundant at the lower levels of the inter-tidal zone, is also sometimes seen on floats in the San Juan area. Unique in structure, its 4 to 16 inch long cylindrical branches have a spongy texture. *Codium* has been used for centuries as food, and also to expel intestinal worms. In Hawaii it is used fresh in relishes. Called chonggak in Korea, it is dried for use as tea.

In the brown alga group there are several common kelps which are a bit tough, but can be used as a soup base or to wrap fish for a clam bake. These occur in the *Laminaria* zone, or deeper on exposed coasts. *Costaria costata,* a striking large kelp, 1½ to 4 feet long, and up to 2 feet wide, has a blistered blade with five strong ribs. Resembling it somewhat is *Agarum finbriatum,* except that it has only one rib. Its blade is perforated and the margin serated and worn. *Cymathere triplicata,* which like *Agarum* does not occur south of Washington, has blades a yard in length and 2 to 3 inches wide, and bears 3 to 5 conspicuous longitudinal folds. *Lessoniopsis litoralis* is a blackish brown kelp with woody stalk with branches producing several narrow mid-ribbed blades up to a yard long. It is found from Alaska to California in surge channels. Also in the *Laminaria* zone is the pompom kelp *Pterygophora californica.* Its long woody stalk forms growth rings, and bears many blades up to a yard in length, which branch off on opposite sides of the stalk Another large seaweed which occurs in the middle to lower intertidal, *Hedophyllum sessile* or sea cabbage, is composed of a large thick brown blade that becomes wrapped around itself, and having no stipe, is attached directly by means of holdfasts to rock. *Scytosiphon lomentaria* also belongs to the brown group though it isn't kelplike, and has a slender flabby tubular growth form. Olive to dark brown, it is generally about 8 inches long and pinched into sausage-shaped segments. It occurs in the lower intertidal zone on both sides of the Pacific. It is used dried, roasted and pulverized for food, and is high in protein. In Japan it is also formed into sheets like nori.

Two very common red seaweeds in the rocky intertidal, which might end up as thickeners (carrageenan) in your cooking, are *Iridaea* and *Gigartina* species. *Gigartina* has a more pleasant taste than *Iridaea.* The two most common *Iridaea* are *I. cordata,* which is large (1 to 3 feet) with thick iridescent blades appearing dark bluish purple; and *I. flaccida,* which is the predominat species of this genus in California. Its blades are less wrinkled than *I. cordata,* measure 12 inches or longer, and are greenish, with purplish lower portions. *Gigartina exasperata* (Turkish towel) forms one or more broad, thick blades up to 12 to 16 feet long, and the edges and flat surfaces are roughened by hundreds of stiff outgrowths. The color is a purplish brick red, and it is somewhat iridescent when wet. *Gigartina* and *Iridaea* are perennials, dying back in winter to a sort of crust. Both are farmed experimentally for a possible carrageenan industry in the Pacific Northwest. *G. papillata*, "grapestone," has been used in pudding type recipes. It is a dull brownish red, up to 6 inches tall, with a stiff rubbery rough texture. This seaweed occurs in an alternating form called *Petroceles*, a dark purple red to black crust on rocks.

Commercial and Imported Sea Vegetables

It would be great if everyone had easy access to sea egetables which grow so abundantly off our rocky shores. But recognizing that fresh seaweeds aren't necessarily in everyone's back yard, it is a comfort to know there are dried or preserved sea vegetables of excellent quality available in health food and other markets. A few recipes for these are included. I regret that in my feverish pursuit of the edible wild sea vegetable, I haven't had time to use the commercial products as much as I wish. Sharon Ann Rhoad's *Cooking With Sea Vegetables* and Juel Andersen's *Sea Green Primer* offer many recipes and much useful information about dried commercial sea vegetables.

A number of seaweeds which are gathered from naturally occurring beds are dried and marketed in the U.S. They include *Chondrus crispus* (Irish moss) and *Palmaria palmata* (dulse), *Alaria* and *Laminaria* from the East Coast; and *Alaria* from Japan (often sold as wakame), *Nereocystis* (bull kelp), *Laminaria* (kelp or kombu), *Postelsia* (sea palm), and *Porphyra* (nori) from the West Coast. Culturing of *Prophyra* has begun in the Pacific Northwest, and we are looking forward to seeing it soon in our markets. *Alaria* is sometimes, sold as a fresh salted product, but, in general sea vegetables are not marketed fresh, because they are so perishable. In Hawaii a number of

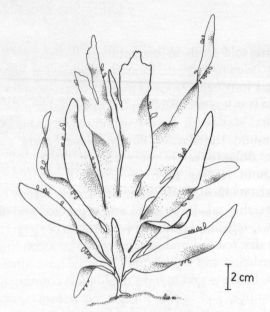

Palmaria palmata (dulse)

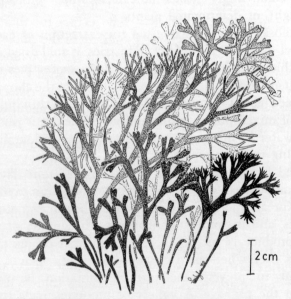

Chondrus crispus (Irish moss)

varieties are sold fresh in markets.

Dulse, *Palmaria palmata*, formerly classified as *Rhodymenia palmata*, has long been enjoyed by East Coast peoples. On the West Coast it is less accessible in the intertidal zone. Gathered from natural stands on New England's rocky shores and in Canada around the Bay of Fundy, Nova Scotia and New Brunswick, dulse is rarely processed to any extent; merely dried (without rinsing in fresh water). Its delicious nutty flavor makes its most popular use as a snack. It may be added to raw vegetable salads, or dried and crumbled and added to soups, stews, relishes, breads, and etc. It can be deep fried as a snack and dry roasted and ground to make a condiment. Its use as a medicine and its nutritive benefits have already been mentioned. Dulse is said to have the highest content of iron of any food source, and is also high in potassium, magnesium, protein and vitamin A. It contains calcium, iodine, phosphorus, plus B_2, B_6, C, E, and trace elements. Dulse should be a deep red-purple color. Light shades indicate improper protection from sunlight, or deteriorated plants.

Irish moss, primarily harvested for extraction of carrageenin, a gel used in a number of industries, is sold dried and used as a thickener in stews, gravies, salads, aspics, pies and puddings. It also has medicinal uses. A half cup of the chopped dried seaweed (about ½ ounce) will gel 4 cups of a thin liquid, or 3 cups of mixed purees, fruits and vegetables. It is rinsed, soaked in water 10 minutes, cooked 20 minutes and strained before adding to the recipe.

In dried form, the Oriental sea vegetables nori (laver), wakame, kombu, agar, arame and hijiki can be found in most Japanese, Korean and Chinese markets, in health or natural foods stores, and in some supermarkets. The quality of the imported product is by no means uniform. Nori quickly deteriorates, even when the package is not visibly open to air. A desiccant to prevent moisture deterioration is often included in the package. A variety of products made from these seaweeds are sold.

In packages of 9 to 10 paper-like sheets, each weighing 3

grams, nori sheets should be naturally dark greenish brown, not dyed. A purple color indicates it may be too old. It is also sold toasted, in which case it is green. Used as they come, or crisped by waving over the flame on a gas range or heating in a medium (300 degree) oven for 2 or 3 minutes, the sheets can then be cut to desired size with scissors or crumbled over stews, casseroles or salads (see recipes for *Porphyra*).

Kombu and wakame should be dark green-black. Light yellow or orange colors are signs of deterioration. Both are packaged in strands, (dashi-kombu comes in wide flat sheets), which may be cut with scissors into appropriate lengths. Freshen by soaking in water 5 to 10 minutes. Both kombu and wakame, made into a powder can be used like salt. Several species of *Laminaria* (there are many names for these kombu types), are used in making soup stock and seasoning. Wakame *(Undaria pinnatifida)* is used in a number of ways (see *Alaria*). Wakame is a superior source of calcium, vitamin B_2 (riboflavin), and niacin. Its nutritional aspects are discussed in Chapter Four, Tables 4 & 5.

Agar, a seaweed gel extracted from several seaweeds belonging to the "Reds," is available in various forms: kanten, strands, powder and flakes. Agar contains calcium, phosphorus, iodine, bromine and trace minerals, with few calories. Varying in their gelling properties, 2 to 4 tablespoons of agars will gel 4 cups of liquid. Agar will not set in the presence of acetic acid (vinegar), or oxalic acid which is found in chocolate, rhubarb, and spinach. For these foods Irish moss may be used. To use kanten bars, merely break, wash, and soak 30 minutes; then dissolve by heating slowly in liquid, stirring constantly. It may be used in a variety of recipes as a thickener for aspics, fruit and vegetable molds, pies, puddings, and jams.

Arame, from another Laminarian, *Eisenia bicyclis,* a large, tough seaweed, dries to a charcoal black color and is chopped into stringlike strips so that it resembles hijiki. Soaked briefly to reconstitute, it is used in soups, salads, tomato dishes and curries. As can be seen in Chapter Four, Table 4, arame is rich in calcium, and contains iron. It keeps well for several years, and thus has been prized as an emergency food.

Hijiki *(Hizikia fusiforme)* is related to *Fucus* and *Sargassum.* Dried, it resembles coarse black tea. A tender and delicious seaweed, hijiki is a powerhouse for vitamins and minerals, especially calcium (see Chapter 3, Table 5). Also a treasure for dieters, it absorbs water and expands up to 4 or 5 times. It is also a delight to watch the tiny flowerlets expand and "come to life" in water. It is very good added to soups and salads, as a stuffing for squash or roll-ups. It may be rehydrated by sautéeing in oil, soy sauce, sugar, cornstarch, and a dash of Worcestershire sauce. Hijiki contains 6 to 7 percent protein, 35 percent carbohydrate, provitamin A, vitamin B, and B_2, and niacin. West Coast *Cystoseira saragassum* or possibly dried *Pelvetiopsis* plants are our nearest possible substitute for this remarkable seaweed.

Table 10

Commercial Sea Vegetable Products

There are 21 varieties of edible sea vegetables in Japan, and as many more in China, Korea and the Philippines. These are made into a great number of products, some of which are available in U.S. markets. Species from other parts of the world are also collected and sold. Below are listed some of those available in U.S. shops.

GREENS

Name	Algal Species	How Sold, Properties, Uses
aonori, aonoriko (Japan)	*Monostroma latissium M. nitidum* and others	fresh, dried, sheets, powder,flakes, salad, seasoning, has high vitamins, iron
awo-nori (Japan)	*Enteromorpha* species	similar to aonori
sea lettuce (worldwide)	*Ulva lactuca, Ulva* species (several)	fresh, dried, powdered, seasoning, high iron, protein, minerals, vitamins
green nori, kelp (U.S.)	any of several greens	powdered green seaweeds, seasoning, vitamins, minerals

BROWNS

Name	Algal Species	How Sold, Properties, Uses
Alaria (U.S.)	Alaria esculenta (east) Alaria marginata (west)	fresh or dried & reconstituted, as vegetable in many recipes, highly nutritious
arame (Japan)	Eisenia bicyclis	dried and chopped into strips for soups, etc. high calcium, potassium, vitamins
bladderwrack (U.S.)	Fucus vesiculosis	chopped, dried for bladderwrack tea, high vitamins, minerals
hijiki (Japan)	Hizikia fusiforme	precooked, dried or salted, many recipes. Vitamins, calcium, protein
kombu (Japan) kelp, tangle (U.S., Europe)	Laminaria species (many)	many products: dried soups, seasonings, vegetables, vitamins, minerals, trace elements
wakame (Japan)	Undaria pinnatifida, Undaria species	several types, dried and salted, fresh, high protein, vitamins, minerals, calcium
seaweed meal kelp meal	Ascophyllum nodosum Alaria esculenta Laminaria species Macrocystis, etc.	minerals, vitamins, trace elements

REDS

Name	Algal Species	How Sold, Properties, Uses
Agar (agar-agar) powder, flakes, or kanten	Many species: Ahnfeltia plicata Gelidium, Gracilaria	thickener, gels, stablizers, emulsifier, in desserts, etc.
dulse (Atlantic and Pacific)	Palmaria palmata	fresh, as salad, vegetables, or dried, snacks; high vitamens, minerals, protein
Irish moss (U.S.)	Chondrus crispus often with Gigartina	Carrageenan, East Coast, fresh, dry, boiled, for thickening puddings and jellies
nori or laver (worldwide)	Porphyra species	several products, dried, sheets, toasted, protein, vitamins, minerals, flavor enhancers

Recipes follow.

Pressure-Cooked Soybeans With Hijiki

1 cup dry soybeans, rinsed and soaked for 2 to 3 hours in 2
  quarts water
2 cups water
thin lemon or lime wedge (opt.)

Drain soybeans, combine with water in pressure cooker.
Pressure cook at 15 pounds for 25 minutes. Remove from heat
and allow to stand for 5 to 10 minutes until pressure returns
to normal. Open and return to stove, and stir in following
ingredients:

3 to 4 tablespoons dry hijiki or slivered kombu, reconstituted
1 tablespoon shoyu or 1½ tablespoons miso
3 tablespoons sesame butter
1 onion or grated carrot, sautéed
2 teaspoons Hot Seas Seasonings (see recipe)

Simmer uncovered for 10 to 15 minutes over low heat. If
necessary, add liquid. Stir from time to time. Grated cheese
may be added just before serving.

Curried Stir Fried Noodles with Tempeh

Modified from the Book of Tempeh; serves 2 or 3.

2 tablespoons vegetable oil
¼ onion, sliced thin
½ cups slivered carrots
1 cup chopped cabbage
¼ cup thinly sliced green onions or scallions
1 to 2 tablespoons dried hijiki, reconstituted and drained
3 ounces buckwheat or wheat noodles, cooked and drained

¼ to ⅜ teaspoon curry powder
2 teaspoons shoyu (natural soy sauce)
¼ teaspoon salt
6 ounces tempeh, cut into ⅜ inch cubes, dipped into seasoning
solution of tamari, garlic and coriander (opt.) and fried
till crisp

Heat wok or cast-iron pan and coat with the oil. Add
onion and carrot and stir fry for 3 minutes. Add cabbage and
green onion and sauté for 2 minutes. Add tempeh and sauté
for a minute or so. Add all remaining ingredients except
tempeh and stir fry vigorously for 1 to 2 minutes more. Mix in
tempeh and remove from heat. Delicious hot or cold.
Note: The original recipe starts with one egg scrambled
in the vegetable oil.

Tofu Hijiki Salad

1 pound firm tofu, drained
6 green onions, chopped
2 stalks celery, diced
2 carrots, grated
¼ bunch parsley
3 tablespoons brewer's yeast
½ cup dried hijiki

Sauce:
Blend together:
¼ cup oil
1 tablespoon lemon juice
2 cloves garlic
2 tablespoons soy sauce
dill and paprika to taste

Soak hijiki in warm water 10 minutes. Drain, cut and dry.
Crumble or mash drained tofu and hijiki. Add remaining
ingredients. Stir the sauce mixture into it. Serve chilled on
green vegetable salad, or use as dip on crackers or chips; or for
stuffing pita bread or sandwiches with avocado and sprouts.

Wakame-Tofu Cashew Cheese Dish

1 head cauliflower cut into bite-sized pieces
8 ounce firm tofu drained and pressed; cut into 1 inch cubes
4 fronds wakame or *Alaria* reconstituted in water and cut into
    bite-sized pieces
1 cup cashews
1 cup water
¼ teaspoon garlic powder
¼ teaspoon celery seed
2 tablespoons lemon juice
2 tablespoons sesame seeds
⅓ cup oil
4 ounce jar pimentos

Steam cauliflowers and tofu over wakame until cauliflower is tender. Combine remaining ingredients except pimento in blender, pouring oil in slowly. Add pimento and heat over low flame in sauce pan. Serve with cauliflower mixture over cooked brown rice.

Scrambled Tofu and Arame

4 tablespoons oil
1 onion chopped
¾ cup arame soaked in water and drained
2 bell peppers
4 to 6 mushrooms, sliced
1 pound tofu, drained and mashed
¼ cup warm water and 1 tablespoon miso, blended together
seasonings to taste such as Italian type, dillweed, rosemary,
    sage, thyme, or turmeric

Sauté onion in oil. Add remaining ingredients in turn, continuing to heat and stir.

Hijiki-Tofu Stir Fry

¾ cup dried hijiki
6 mushrooms
2 carrots
½ pound green beans
2 tablespoons oil
3 tablespoons tamari (soy sauce)
2 tablespoons barley malt
1 pound firm tofu, cut into cubes and marinaded

Marinade: 3 parts oil, 2 parts tamari, 1 part cider vinegar, piece ginger, sesame seeds

Soak hijiki 15 minutes. Soften mushrooms if dried in 1 cup hot water. Trim stems and cut tops into slivers. Slice carrots and beans. Heat oil, and stir fry ingredients. Add marinaded tofu, and serve with rice.

No Sugar Cranberry Sauce

1 tablespoon raisins
2½ tablespoons agar flakes
2½ cups apple juice or cider
3 cups cranberries

Soak raisins and agar flakes in apple juice. And cranberries, bring to boil, and cook over low flame 10 minutes or until cranberries are soft. Pour into mold or serving dish. Cool, and refrigerate.

Fresh Fruit Freezer Jam

Delicious, easy to prepare, and very low in sugar.

3 cups mashed fruit at room temperature (seeded berries O.K.)
1 tablespoon lemon juice
½ cup cold water
3½ tablespoons agar flakes
¾ cups sugar, or ½ cup honey (more or less to taste)

Stir lemon juice into fruit. Place water in sauce pan and stir in agar flakes. Allow to soak 1 minute, then bring to simmer over medium-low heat, stirring 2 minutes, until agar is completely dissolved. Stir in honey or sugar. Pour agar-honey mixture slowly into mashed fruit, stirring until completely mixed. (Do not add the fruit to the agar.) Pour into clean jars, leaving ¾ inch headspace for half pint jars and 1 inch for pints. Freeze. Yields 4 to 4½ cups jam.

Sushi

Don't be intimidated! These are really easy to make. Use commercial nori, as it makes neat rolls.

3 sheets nori, toasted over burner until they turn bright green, but are still flexible
3½ cups sushi rice (see below)
½ cucumber, cut into long 18 inch strips
strips of Paper Thin Omelets (below)
strips of carrot, thin, cut like cucumber

Place 1 sheet of nori on a sudare (bamboo mat) or dry dishcloth. Spread ⅓ of the rice evenly over the nori, leaving a 1 inch wide strip at the far edge. Place ⅓ of cucumber strips, and a strip or two of carrot and egg in a row about 2 inches from the near edge of the nori. Roll up the nori and moisten edge with water to seal. Let sit a couple of minutes to let the nori moisten. Cut the roll crosswise into 10 small discs. (Wipe knife with moist cloth to prevent sticking.) Repeat with remaining ingredients.

Sushi Rice:
1 cup brown rice or niko-niko Japanese rice, soak in 1⅓ cups water overnight in a heavy 2 to 4 quart pot

Bring soaked rice to boil, reduce heat to low and simer 40 to 50 minutes. Remove from heat and allow to stand 5 minutes. Transfer hot rice to wooden bowl, and immediately sprinkle with dressing. Mix the rice vigorously while fanning it, to cool it as quickly as possible. Do this for about 3 minutes, then allow to cool to room temperature.

Vinegar Dressings:
2⅓ tablespoons vinegar
2 teaspoons honey
½ teaspoon salt

For unsweetened sushi rice:
4 tablespoons vinegar
1½ teaspoon salt

Paper Thin Omelets:
2 eggs
½ teaspoon ground, roasted sesame seeds
⅛ teaspoon salt
½ to 1 teaspoon oil

Heat skillet and lightly coat with oil, pouring off any excess. Mix remaining ingredients. Pour about ¼ of this mixture into the skillet, swishing it around quickly so that it covers the bottom of the pan. Cook over high heat for about 20 to 30 seconds on one side only, to form a thin omelet. Transfer to plate and allow to cool. Repeat 4 times.

Part III

Seaweeds in Society

CHAPTER SIX

SEAWEED HARVEST
AND CULTIVATION LAWS

The individual seaweed forager faces relatively few legal restrictions for harvesting seaweeds. Since each state varies in laws pertaining to ownership and development of tidelands, it is important for the forager to keep this in mind should his adventures lead him to different coastal states.

In Alaska, for example, seaweed with herring roe attached to it is in commercial demand for export to Japan, where it is a gourmet food item. For this reason, the State of Alaska regulates the harvest of certain species of seaweed in some areas. Otherwise there are virtually no regulations or restrictions on the harvest of seaweeds for the individual, but a permit is required for commerical harvesting.

In the state of Washington, the Department of Natural Resources acts as proprietary agent for the public ownership of bedlands and tidelands. Seaweeds on privately owned or leased tidelands belong to the owner or leasee. Up to fifty pounds per year may be taken on state owned aquatic lands. No more than fifty percent of an annual species or seventy-five percent of a perennial species may be taken in any one acre area. Commercial harvesting is by permit only. Fourteen species are regulated, and maximum free-harvest limits are set for these species. Payment of a royalty, dependent on species, quantity and use, is a condition of the permit. Plants must be removed in a manner to assure their regeneration. Permits are required from several agencies for culturing seaweed on state owned bedlands. There are two nori farms fully permited, and two in process. No harvesting permits for cultured nori have been issued so far.

In Oregon, where private ownership of coastal land is restricted to above the upper tidal levels, public access is unrestricted. Little legislation exists regarding the harvest of seaweed for personal use. There is, at present, no commercial harvesting, and no provision for leasing intertidal or tidelands for kelp harvest. Commercial harvest from offshore beds does require a lease.

The forager in California needs a permit from the Department of Parks and Recreation to collect seaweeds in a state park. Also, should any animals be removed with the seaweeds, you are expected to have both a fishing license and collecting permit from the State Department of Fish and Game. The Department of Fish and Game regulates seaweed harvesting, licensing and leasing arrangements for cultivation of a number of commercially valuable seaweed. The cultivator of algae must also comply with Federal laws which deal with navigation.

In Hawaii there are few restrictions to harvesting seaweed, known locally as "limu." Collecting is prohibited on several marine life conservation districts. Commercial collectors need a commercial fishing license and a gross income license to sell their limu. In 1981 the total reported harvest was approximately 9,000 pounds with a wholesale value of $18,860. Provision for leasing tidelands for aquacultural purposes is now under consideration by the Legislature.

In British Columbia the seaweed resources are managed and administered by the Provincial Government. Individuals gathering seaweeds for their own use are not subject to fees or regulations. Commercial harvesters must pay license and processing fees. At present there are twenty-seven licensed harvesters; twenty-six harvest *Macrocystis* for the herring roe-on-kelp industry; and one harvests *Porphyra* (nori) for the edible seaweed market. Several pilot scale studies are investigating the feasibility of culturing *Laminaria groenlandica* and *Cymathere triplicata* for the kombu market. Research is underway to explore the potential of several other species. Marine plant culture operation requires permits from several agencies.

On the Atlantic coast side of the U.S., Maine is apparently the only state where there is sufficient seaweed to support extensive commercial harvesting. There is at present no provision for aquaculture leases for seaweed. A $13 harvesting fee and $25 selling fee is required for harvest of *Chondrus crispus* (Irish moss). For the non-commercial harvester, there are no restrictions, licensing or fees.

New Hampshire restricts seaweed harvest to residents only, in daylight hours. No out of state sales are allowed. Residents are limited to 3 bushels per day, and the harvest must be done by cutting, not by pulling off the holdfasts. Harvesting on private lands is by owner permission.

In Massachusetts there are no licensing or fee requirements, but permission from the Director of Marine Fisheries is needed for mechanical harvest of *Chondrus crispus* (Irish moss). At present there are two approvals issued for this harvest.

Most of the remaining eastern U.S. coastal states have no licensing or fee requirements and no restrictions. Apparently the quantity of seaweed there is now very limited. Fishery managers in Maryland have noted an unexplained drastic decline in seaweed in the Chesapeake Bay system, which is being studied. Biologists there are alarmed because the seaweed had formerly provided a valuable nursery ground for fish and a major attraction for wintering waterfowl.

An examination of the legal hurdles with which a harvester or cultivator of seaweeds must comply, show that present laws are inadequate. These laws developed from ancient customs pertaining to hunting and gathering on common grounds, which are antithetic to our concept of private ownership in agriculture. A salmon rancher, for instance, must make investments in a resource without much protection or assurance that the resource will not be claimed by another harvester. In the case of the seaweed cultivator, the crop will not swim away, but there is no permanent legal claim to the property involved.

Public policy issues must be addressed. Fencing of large areas of tidelands and open ocean would be impractical and probably objectionable to most people. But since there are many conflicts between traditional ocean uses and widescale development of seaweed culture, value judgements will be necessary to resolve them.

One way or another, this resource will eventually be developed. It is important to prevent the consequences of haphazard and irresponsible development. Good laws must be formulated which will preserve beauty, enjoyment and ecological stability of the coast. The complicated Law of the Sea Treaty, which has been developing in the United Nations for many years, is not yet in force. It is hoped that the sea and seabed will be internationally regulated, and the concept of these resources as the "common heritage of mankind" will be fulfilled.

> Come, friends who plow the sea,
>   Truce to navigation,
>   Take another station;
> Let's vary piracee
>   With a little burglaree.

Patience by Sir William Schwerek Gilbert

CHAPTER SEVEN

SEAWEEDS FOR FERTILIZER

Seaweeds have had a long and important history of increasing soil fertility and improving soil composition. The Romans used them for manure as well as animal fodder. Scotland's sandy soils profited from the use of seaweed. On the barren rocks of the Aran Islands, Ireland, seaweeds used in combination with pulverized rocks, produced soil for the raising of potatoes. In Brittany fresh coralline algae, called marl, was used directly for farming and in the making of lime. Farms along the Brittany and Normandy coasts of France, known as the "golden belt," relied for many centuries on seaweed ("wrack") for their productivity. In fact, the farmers had a saying, "No wrack, no grain."

Seaweed fertilizer is complex, containing all major and minor plant nutrients, several auxins, gibberellins, cytokinin, vitamins, chelating agents and soil conditioners. Having the advantage of containing no weed seeds and soil micro-organisms, such as fungus spores, seaweed is comparable to barnyard manure in fertilizing capacity, but contains more potassium salts, less phosphorus and about the same proportion of nitrogen. For this reason, it is particularly beneficial for root crops such as beets and potatoes. Most of the potassium salts are water soluble and therefore immediately available for plant use, whereas the nitrogen and phosphoric acid are released slowly and become available only on decay of the seaweed material. An inherent value of seaweed as a fertilizer lies in its providing trace nutrients as well as organic growth substance. Commercial chemical fertilizers are currently recognized to be lacking in certain trace elements, often needed in minute quantities. Cultivated soil is likely to become impoverished if certain trace elements are gradually used up by crops or leached out.

Seaweed extracts as fertilizer produce many beneficial results beside increased crop yields. They improve seed germination, increase hardiness of plants to frost and insect and fungal attacks, and increase uptake of inorganic constituents from the soil.

Table 11 compares fresh seaweed and farmyard manure in organic matter, nitrogen, phosphorus and potassium (from W. A. Stephanson, *Seaweed in Agriculture and Horticulture.* London, Faber and Faber. 1968.).

Making Your Own
Seaweed Compost & Liquid Fertilizer

The seaweed forager who also gardens will find gathering of the abundant cast-up seaweed for fertilizer well worth the trouble. To minimize the effort of hauling it, it is useful to recall that dry seaweed is only one-tenth the weight of wet. So, if possible, allow it to dry first on the beach, especially if it must be hauled up a cliff. At low tide, gather up the loose seaweed and carry it to a high spot where incoming tides will not reach it. Then in a day or two it will be much lighter and can be more easily carried to the garden. A liquid fertilizer is made by allowing the rotting seaweed to stand in a pail of water. The liquid, poured off when needed, fertilizes house plants (if you can stand the odor!) or anything in the garden. Foliar application may be accomplished by applying the liquid with a sprayer.

The seaweed, often a mix of many species of algae plus sea grasses, shells, and chitinous materials rich in minerals and

218 – Sea Vegetables

organic material, does not need to be rinsed with fresh water for use as fertilizer. Since marine algae are a bit low in phosphorus when compared to plant and animal manures or commercial fertilizers, it is helpful to include sea grasses (eelgrass, *Zostera*, and surf grass, *Phyllospadix*,) which are high in phosphorus. Marine animal shell and skeletal material may also be applied to insure a product complete in plant nutrients.

Marine algae and sea grasses break down very quickly to release their minerals into the soil. Application a few weeks or months before planting will allow maximum breakdown and benefit to soil structure, but seaweed may also be applied during the growing season with no danger of "burning." Seaweed, used as compost or as liquid fertilizer, adequately provides minerals, plus essential trace elements and useful soil conditioners and growth stimulants; benefits which are often not found in other fertilizers. The nicest bonus – no weed seeds in seaweed compost to plague the gardener later!

The following Table 11 compares fresh seaweed and farmyard manure in organic matter, nitrogen, phosphorus and potassium (from W. A. Stephanson, *Seaweed in Agriculture and Horticulture.* London, Faber and Faber. 1968.).

Table 11

Fertilizer Analysis

Analysis (in pounds) of one ton of fertilizer material.

	Farmyard Manure	Fresh Seaweed
organic matter	380	400
nitrogen	11	11
phosphorus	6	2
potassium	15	27

CHAPTER EIGHT

SEAWEEDS AS ANIMAL FODDER

It may come as a surprise to the reader that in coastal areas many different animals seek out seaweed. Apparently it not only supplies needed minerals, but in times of scarcity serves for food energy. Domestic animals since ancient times have been fed fresh seaweed or seaweed meal (mostly kelps) as a supplement with good results. Once the world's record for milk production was won by the Overbrook dairy herd in the U.S., which was fed with dried seaweed.

The abundant minerals and vitamins of seaweeds are retained very well in processing procedures. Though low in protein and calories, seaweed meal can be used as part or all of the rations for ruminants (cattle and sheep) and as a supplement for horses, pigs and chickens to provide needed vitamins, minerals, trace elements, and roughage; and reduce incidence of parasites and bacterial disease. The health of animals is often improved, thereby increasing the production and quality of meat, eggs, milk and wool.

CHAPTER NINE

SEAWEEDS
IN THE MEDICINE CHEST

In addition to their marvelous contribution to nutrition, the nearly 6,500 species of seaweeds in the world's seas and oceans represent an almost limitless reserve of natural biologically active and potentially useful pharmaceutical products. Long valued in folk medicine, marine plants, having adapted to a different environment, contain an number of rare properties and elements extremely important to modern medicine, although in some cases research is still in an early stage. Ancient Chinese pharmacology suggested biomedical benefits from algae in the cure of many diseases, including cancer, dropsy and menstrual disorders. Seaweeds have successfuly been used, as well, in treatment of worms, goiter, kidney disease, reducing blood cholesterol and hypertension, ulcers, and radioactive strontium poisoning. Nausea, indigestion, seasickness, heart ailments, rheumatism, influenza, mumps, hay fever, obesity, nervous dyspepsia, high blood pressure, and constipation are among several other ailments treated by seaweeds. It has long been believed, especially by the Japanese and Chinese, that the use of seaweed can prevent, relieve and cure a variety of human diseases and prolong life. Refer to Table 12 for an indepth review of which seaweeds are used to cure or alleviate certain widespread illnesses.

Marine Algae In Pharmacy & Health

The following account of the healing properties of *Nereocystis* (bull kelp) recently came to me from kayakers whom we met on a trip in British Columbia. Jim and Corrine Berta, while camping on Vargas Island, west of Vancouver Island, made *Nereocystis* kelp pickles on the beach (testing some of my recipes). Hurrying before dark to get their gear packed, Jim tried to extinguish the fire with the big pot of water they had used for canning. He slipped, spilling the water on the extremely hot sand, causing an explosion of steam.

Jim writes: "The backs of both my hands were severely burned (second degree burns). I instantly had a couple of flashes go through my mind. I first remembered that we decided not to bring a first aid kit because we wanted to travel light and we weren't that far into a wilderness area. Second, I remembered reading that the Nootka People used to use the gel in the *Fucus* sacs for minor cuts. Third, I remembered thinking as I handled the kelp how the "gooey" substance which came from the slices reminded me of aloe vera, which has been used by people for centuries for burns.

"I was in great pain as these thoughts were going through my mind. We had a couple of pieces of cut kelp which we hadn't used. I began to rub the gooey sliced surface on the backs of my hands, and as I did, the pain was gone immediately. I couldn't believe it! I found that the *Nereocystis* gave temporary relief at first; and I had to rub it on about once every minute for about five minutes. After about 10 minutes I didn't have to rub the kelp on nearly so often. In the next hour I only used the kelp 2 or 3 times more, when I felt the pain. After about an hour the pain didn't return. But the most amazing thing was that blisters never developed! In wilderness first aid situations I have seen many such burns. I was certain that they were second degree, and would later develop huge water blisters.

"My hand lost all painful sensitivity to touch. I even packed my gear into the kayak and paddled home without any pain. In fact, I even forgot about my burned hands while I was paddling.

"The next day as I related this story to friends, I noticed that the injured areas on my hands had become a strange reddish purple color, but there was no pain or any other sign or symptom. Four or five days later large patches of dark brown skin began peeling from these areas. The peeling skin was very unusual in its thickness, and the new skin underneath was normal in color – none of the pink new skin which usually occurs after a burn!

"In the past I have used two different first aid ointments for wilderness burn victims. These ointments are used in industrial first aid. Neither of these ointments seemed to assist the healing process like the kelp did for me. Also the kelp is water soluble, which is an essential quality for a burn medication."

Jim hopes that medical research will develop the potential of this remarkable seaweed gel, so that the healing substance will be available to aid other burn victims.

Table 12

Marine Algae
In Modern & Folk Medicine

GREEN ALGAE (Chlorophyta)

	Where Used	Uses
Acetabularia major	S.E. Asia	gallstone treatment
Caulerpa species		food
C. lamourouxii & *C. racemosa*		toxic? peppery taste, mild anesthetic in mouth— neuotropic uses
Cladophora glomerata		burns treatment
Codium species		vermifuge, especially for *Ascaris*
Cymapolia barbata		antibiotic; also for *Salmonella gallinarium* in chickens
Enteromorpha	Japan	wens, hermorrhoids, stomach diseases
Pleurococcus naegelli		antibiotic against *Staph.* and *Strep.*, also parasites and skin disease
Rhizodonium rivulare		vermifuge and healing wounds
Trentipohlea iolithus		skin diseases
Ulva lactuca		gout, astringent, scrofula
U. penniformis	Siberia	medical preparations
U. pertusa	China	anthelmintic (vermifuge)

BROWN ALGAE (Phaeophyta)

	Where Used	Uses
Analipus japonicus		food; hypotensive
Ascophyllum nodosum		obesity, rheumatism, sprains
Chordaria flagelliformis	E. Asia, Kamchatka	food; anticoagulant
Cutleria multifida		gastric ulcers
Cystoseira barbata	Adriatic & Black Sea	lipolytic and hypoglycemic
Dictyopteris polypodioides	Mediterranean	lung disease and scrofula

	Where Used	**Uses**
Darvillea antarctica	Maoris in N. Zealand	scabies, vermifuge
Eisenia bicyclis (arame)		food, anti-inflamatory & anti-curare, gynecological diseases
Eisenia & Eclonia	Japan	(added to bath water), palsy and hypertension
Fucus esculentus	Russia	in sweets; for sclerosis and thyroid disturbance
F. Gardneri		reducing plasma cholesterin
F. vesiculosis		iodine; for obesity, goiter, Basido's disease
Fucus species		blood anticoagulant
F. visiculosus tostus		scrofulosis and goiter
Laminaria species	Japan & China	food; lowering blood pressure, Fucosterol reduces blood cholesterol
L. saccharina	Russia	constipation, goiter, arteriosclerosis
L. angustata		arteriosclerosis, hypertension
L. hyperboria and *L. digitata*		surgery and gynecology
L. japonica	China	cooling, blood cleaning, hypothyroidism
"	Japan	neuroses, palsy, anti-hypertensive, edema
Macrocystis pyrifera	U.S.	kelp tablets for vitamins, minerals, pregnancy anemia
Nematocystic dicipiens	Japan	wens and swelling
Nereocystis leutkeana	N.A. Indians	medicine
Sargassum confusum		Sargaline, reduces blood sugar level
S. fusiforma and *S. thumbergi*	China	cooling and blood cleaning, glandular weakness, apoplexy, blood pressure, anthelmintic
S liniifolium	India	urinary troubles and calculous diseases
S. muticum		Sargasterol, reducing blood plasma and cholesterol level

	Where Used	Uses
S. natans	S. America	goiter and renal disorders
S. vulgare		increases serum lipolytic activity, hypoglycemic and antilipemic
Stilophora rhizoides	Mediterranean	lung diseases and scrofula
Undaria pinnatifida (wakame)	Japan	food; cures nicotine poisoning, high blood pressure, arterial sclerosis, liver complaints, blood cleansing after childbirth

RED ALGAE (Rhodophyta)

	Where Used	Uses
Alsidium helminthochorton (corsican moss)		anthelmintic
Centroceras clavulatum	East Asia	medicine
Ceramium loureirii	Pacific	chest diseases
C. rubrum		dye in cosmetics
Chondria armata	Japan & S. E. Asia	anthelmintic for roundworm, pinworm, also flies (Domoic acid)
Ch. littoralis		antibiotic against *E. coli* and *Candida albicans*
Ch. oppositicloda		antibiotic against *Staph. aureus* and *Candida albicans* (chondriol & cycloeudesmol)
Chondria sanguinea and *Ch. vermixularis*	Brazil	anthelmintic, and indigestion
Chondrus crispus with *Gigartina stellata* (Irish moss)		respiratory ailments, mucilage against diarrhea, dysentery, gastric ulcers, colds
Constantinea simplex		potential prevent/treat *Herpes simplex*
Corallina species		vermifuge, burns, gastritis, diarrhea
C. rubens		lipolytic, hypoglycemic, and anhelmintic
Cryptosiphonia woodii		potential prevent/treat *Herpes simplex*
Delesseria sanguinea		blood anticoagulant

	Where Used	**Uses**
Dictyoptrii plagiogramma	Hawaii	antilipemic
Digenea simplex	China	anthelmentic (Ascaris)
Dilsea edulus		blood anticoagulent
Eucheuma species	Philippines	cough remedy
Farlowia mollis		potential prevent/treat Herpes simplex
Gelidium cartilageneum	Japan	colds and scrofula
G. latifolium		antilipemic
Gracilaria confervoides		antilipemic and for colds
Grateloupia species		antithelmintics
Hypnea japonica		increase calcium uptake in bones
H. musciformes	Greece, Turkey, Indonesia	vermifuge (anthelmentic)
H. nidifica	Hawaii	stomach treatment
Iridaea flaccida		blood anticoagulant
Lithothamnion species		water filters & neutralizer
Phyllophora nervosa	Turkey	antilipemic & anticoagulant
Plocamium coccineum		red pigment, cosmetics
Polysiphonia subulifera		increases serum lipolytic activity
Porphyra atropurpurea	Japan	beriberi and wens
Porphyra atropurpurea		poultices and cataplasms
P. columbina	N. Zealand, Maoris	aperient
Pterocladia capillaceae		lipolytic and hypoglycemic
Rhodymenia indica	East Asia	vermifuge
Sphaerococus cartilageneus	China	medicament

Information from Hoppe, Heinz, A., *Marine Algae and Their Products and Constituents in Pharmacy*, 1979; and Hoppe, Heinz, A., T. Levring, and Y. Tanaka, Editors, *Marine Algae in Pharmaceutical Science*. Also Arasaki, Seibin and Teruko, *Vegetables From The Sea*, Japan Publications, Inc., 1983.

CHAPTER TEN

SEAWEED
COLLECTIONS & STATIONERY

Many seaweed fanciers enjoy preparing pressed and dried seaweed specimens, which serve as a permanent record of a collection of observation and as a reference for identification of later collections. From these beautiful collections, the smaller forms often make interesting decorations for note cards or stationery. These dried specimens are prepared by spreading a wet seaweed specimen of appropriate size on a piece of high quality paper, such as biology drawing paper, herbarium paper or card weight paper. Seaweeds contain abundant sticky substances to glue themselves to the paper. Stationery weight paper will also work, but sometimes becomes messy looking. Index cards may be used for small specimens and for note cards.

Mounting is best accomplished in a broad shallow pan or tray large enough to accommodate the size of the sheet of paper used. Pour seawater in the tray to fully immerse specimen. Float the specimen out of the tray and on to the paper, and then lift the paper carefully allowing the water to drain off, leaving the specimen spread out artistically on the paper. A medicine dropper is useful in arranging specimens and removing excess water. Use small tools such as a tweezer or toothpicks to arrange the seaweed; trim any excess. The sheet or card with the specimen is then placed on dry felt or blotter and covered either with a piece of cloth or piece of waxed paper. The process is repeated and blotters stacked,

with newspapers and corrugated cardboard between specimens to provide ventilation and hasten the drying.

The bundle is secured by means of a board and heavy
weights, or a standard plant press frame with straps, to keep
the specimens flat. The blotters, corrugated cardboaad, and
papers must be changed daily until the specimens are dry.
A blowing heat source hastens drying, but excessive heat may
cause the specimens to become brittle.

A serious collector will label the sheet with the name of
the seaweed, the date and place of collection, the name of the
collector and any pertinent field notes.

Coastal postals, note cards and stationery from the sea.

SEAWEED SUPPLIERS

American Sea Vegetable Co.   *Nori cultivator.*
John Olson
P.O. Box 515
Coupeville, WA 98239

Applied Phycology Forum   *Quarterly newsletter,*
P.O. Box 11157   *$5.00 subscription.*
Boulder, CO 80301

Atlantic Mariculture LTD   *Dulse and kelp products.*
Castalia, Grand Manan
New Brunswick, Canada EOG ILO

Maine Coast Sea Vegetables   *Nori, kelp, Alaria, Irish*
Shepard and Linnette Erhart   *moss, dulse suppliers.*
Franklin, ME 04634

Mendocino Sea Vegetable Co.   *Porphyra, Alaria, Lamin-*
John and Eleanor Lewallen   *aria, Palmaria, sea palm*
P.O. Box 372   *fronds, Ulva, Gigartina,*
Navarro, CA 95463   *and recipe booklet.*

New Channel Nori Farms   *Nori culture, several*
Zoology NJ-15   *varieties of local wild*
University of Washington   *sea vegetables.*
Seattle, WA 98195

New England Sea Vegetables   *Alaria, Palmaria, Lamin-*
Larch and Jan Hanson   *aria, Porphyra, Chon-*
Box 15   *drus, and recipe booklet.*
Steuben, MA 04680

NW Nori Growers Assn.
David & Anne Berfield
9416 Olson Rd.
Bainbridge Island, WA 98110

Nori products.

Ocean Energy
Matthew Hodel
2268 Juan Pablo
Santa Cruz, CA 95062

Porphyra, Alaria, Nereocystis, Nereocystis pickles, Postelsia, Palmaria.

Olympia Sea Gardens, Inc.
Mark C. Bishop
P.O. Box 236
Sequim, WA 98382

Alaria, Porphyra, Ulva, Enteromorpha, sushi, nori sheets.

Oregon Sea Vegetables
Evelyn McConnaughey
1653 Fairmount Blvd.
Eugene, OR 97403

Alaria, Porphyra (several species), Ulva, recipe booklets and notecards.

**Pacific Northwest Nori
    Growers Assn.**
c/o Dr. Thomas Mumford
Washington Dept. of Nat. Resources
Marine Land Management EX-12
Public Lands Bldg.
Olympia, WA 98504

Rising Tide Sea Vegetables
Kate Marianchild
P.O. Box 228
Philo, CA 95466

Porphyra, Alaria, Ulva, Palmaria, Laminaria.

West Brae
4240 Hollis Ave.
Emeryville, CA 94662

Alaria, kelp, agar; and many other products.

BIBLIOGRAPHY

Abbott, I. and E. H. Williamson. *Limu – An Ethnobotanical Study of Some Edible Hawaiian Seaweeds.* Lawai (Hawaii): Pacific Tropical Botannical Garden. 1974.

Abbott, I. and E. Yale Dawson. *How to Know the Seaweeds. The Pictured Key Nature Series.* Second Edition. William C. Brown Publishers. Dubuque, Iowa. 1956.

Abbott, I. A. and G. J. Hollenberg. *Marine Algae of California.* Stanford University Press, Stanford. 1976.

Anderson, Juel and Richard Ford. *The Sea Green Primer.* Creative Arts Communications, Berkeley, California. 1983.

Arasaki, Seibin and Teruko, *Vegetables from the Sea.* Japan Publications, Inc., Tokyo, Japan. 1983.

Bardach, John, H. Ryther, and William O. McLarney. *Aquaculture – The Farming and Husbandry of Freshwater and Marine Organisms.* John Wiley & Sons, New York. 1972.

Bold, Harold C. and Michael I. Wynne. *Introduction to the Algae, Structure and Reproduction.* Prentice Hall, Inglewood Cliff, New Jersey. 1975.

Boney, A. D. "Aspects of the Biology of the Seaweeds of Economic Importance," *Advanced Marine Biology.* First edition. Russell. Vol. 3, pp. 105 – 253. 1965.

Borgese, Elisabeth Mann. *Seafarm, The Story of Aquaculture.* Harry N. Abrams, Inc., New York. 1977.

Chapman, Valentine J. *Seaweeds and their Uses.* Second edition. Halsted, New York. 1970.

Dawes, Clinton J. *Marine Botany.* John Wiley & Sons, Inc., New York. 1981.

Dawson, Elmer Y. *Marine Botany: An Introduction.* Holt, Rinehart and Winston, New York. 1966.

Dawson, Elmer Y. and Michael S. Foster. *Seashore Plants of California.* University of California Press. 1982.

Druehl, L. D. "Past, Present and Future of the Seaweed Industry," *Underwater. J. Inf. Bull.* Vol. 4, no. 5, pp. 182 – 191. 1972.

Fortner, Heather J. "The Limu Eater – a cookbook of Hawaiian Seaweed." *Sea Grant Miscellaneous Report UNIHI SEA-GRANT.* MR-79-01. 1978.

Fryer, Lee and D. Simons, *Food Power from the Sea: The Seaweed Story.* Mason Charter, New York. 1977.

Geary, L. "Seaweed Washed Ashore: Collecting and Preserving the Plants of the Sea," *Oceans.* Vol. 13, pp. 6 – 10. March/April 1980.

Gosner, Kenneth L. *The Peterson Field Guide Series, no. 24. A Field Guide to the Atlantic Seashore.* Houghton Mifflin Company, Boston. 1979.

Guberlet, Muriel Lewin. *Seaweeds at Ebb Tide.* University of Washington Press, Seattle. 1956.

Hanson, Larch. *Edible Sea Vegetables of the New England Coast.* Box 15, Steuben, Maine 04680.

Hoppe, H. A. *Marine Algae in Pharmaceutical Science.* De Gruyter and Co., Berlin and New York. 1979.

Hunter, C. J. "Edible Seaweeds – Survey of the Industry and Prospects for Farming the Pacific Northwest," *Marine Fish Review.* Vol. 37, no. 2, pp. 19 – 26. 1975.

Idyll, C. P. *The Sea Against Hunger.* Thomas Y. Corwell Co., New York. 1978.

Kozloff, Eugene N. *Seashore Life of the Northern Pacific Coast.* University of Washington Press. Seattle, WA. 1983.

Krauss, R. W., Ed. *The Marine Plant Biomass of the Pacific Northest Coast. A Potential Economic Resource.* OSU Press, Corvallis, Oregon. 1978.

Lappé, Francis Moore. *Diet for a Small Planet.* Ballantine Books, Inc., New York. 1971, 75 and 82.

Lee, Thomas F. *The Seaweed Handbook: An Illustrated Guide to Seaweeds from North Carolina to the Arctic.* Mariners' Press, Boston. 1977.

Levring, T., H. A. Hoppe, and O. J. Schmid. *Marine Algae – A Survey of Research and Utilization.* De Gryuter and Co., Hamburg, Germany. 1969.

Lewallen, Eleanor and John. *The Sea Vegetable Gourmet Cookbook and Forager's Guide.* P.O. Box 372, Navarro, CA 95463. 1983.

McKee, Alexander. *Farming the Sea.* Crowell, New York. 1969.

Madlener, J. C. *The Sea Vegetable Book.* Clardon N. Potter, Inc., New York. 1977.

_____. *The Sea Vegetable Gelatin Cookbook and Field Guide.* Woodbridge Press. 1981.

Major, Alan. *The Book of Seaweed.* Gordon and Cremonesi, London and New York. 1977.

Matthews, S. W. "New World of the Ocean," *National Geographic.* Vol. 160, no. 6. December 1981.

Michanek, G. "Seaweed Resources for Pharmaceutical Uses," *Marine Algae in Pharmaceutical Service.* (Edited by H. A. Hoppe, and Lerning and Y. Tanaka.) De Gruyter, Berlin. 1979.

Miura, Akio. "Seaweed Cultivation: Present Practices and Potentials," *Ocean Yearbook.* Vol. 2, pp. 57 – 68. Borgese, E. M. and M. Ginsburg, Eds. University of Chicago Press. 1980.

Mumford, Thomas F. Jr. "Seaweed Culture in Washington and British Columbia: Potential and Practice,"*International Symposium on Coastal Pacific Marine Life.* Proceedings Oct. 15 – 16, 1979. Western Washington University, Bellingham. pp. 13 – 30. 1980.

Norton, Reggi, and Martha Wagner. *The Soy of Cooking.* White Crane, Eugene, Oregon. 1980.

Palmer, E. F. "The Marine Algae – In the Sea's Weeds May Lie the Future's Insurance Against Starvation," *Natural History.* 1961.

Piattelli, Mario. "Neptunes Pharmacopaeia," *UNESCO Courier.* Vol. 32, pp. 29 – 31. July 1979.

Pharmaceutical Uses of Seaweeds presented in the Proceedings of 9th International Seaweed Symposium. Santa Barbara,

California. Arne Jensen and Janet R. Stein, Editors. Published by Science Press as supplement to *Botanica Marina.* 1977.

Plotkin, J. "Seaweed: Manure, Mulch and Fertilizer Free From The Sea," *Organic Garden and Farm.* Vol. 24, pp. 148 – 149. Spring 1977.

Rhee, Katherine C. "Soil Improving with Seaweed," *Organic Gardening and Farming.* Vol. 19, pp. 56 – 59. August 1972.

Rhoads, Sharon Ann. *Cooking with Sea Vegetables.* Autumn Press, Brookline, Mass. 1978.

Scagel, R. F. "Marine Plant Resources of British Columbia," *Fish Res. Board, Canada, Bull. No. 127.* Board of Canada. 1961.

――――――. *Guide to Common Seaweeds of British Columbia. Handbook No. 27.* British Columbia Provincial Museum, Dept. of Recreation and Conservation, Victoria B.C. 1967.

Shurtleff, W. and Aoyagi. *The Book of Tofu, Food for Mankind.* Vol. 1. Autumn Press. Revised Ballantine Books, New York. 1975.

"Spirulina: Protein of the Future," *Mother Earth News.* Vol 68, pp. 180 – 181. March/April 1981.

Stephenson, W. A. *Seaweed in Agriculture and Horticulture.* Faber and Faber, London. 1968.

Stoner, M. "Sea Vegetables: Using the Sea's Harvest," *Organic Garden and Farm.* Vol. 19, pp. 73 – 76. December 1972.

"Therapeutic Seaweed," *Oceanology Int.* Vol. 22, May/June 1969.

Waaland, J. Robert. *Common Seaweeds of the Pacific Coast.* Pacific Search Press/Nature. 1977.

Zimmerman, R. "Seaweed Turns Sand Into Fertile Soil," *Organic Garden and Farm.* Vol. 20, pp. 85 – 86. December 1973.

See also: *Proceedings of the International Seaweed Symposia, First through Tenth.*

RECIPE INDEX

Soups

Main Dishes

Breads

Vegetables

Egg & Cheese

Pickles

Miscellaneous